Praise for Awakening by

"Too many Western Christians have limited vision both when they read the Scriptures and when they read the headlines. God has been and is today at work in his world! Matt Brown offers stirring examples and pointed advice on being a part of God's great movement on earth. Join the movement!"

> —**Alvin L. Reid,** professor of evangelism and student ministry, Bailey Smith Chair of Evangelism, Southeastern Baptist Theological Seminary

"God is up to something, and it's big. *Awakening* makes that clear. The stories Matt Brown tells from around the world open your eyes to what God is up to, and they open the eyes of your heart to what God might want to do in you too. Matt isn't saying, 'look what the world has come to,' he's telling us 'what has come to the world.' Christ has come, and he is on the move like never before!"

> —**David Drury,** Chief of Staff, the Wesleyan Church International Headquarters, author or co-author of half a dozen books, including *Being Dad, SoulShift,* and *Ageless Faith*

"This book is a drink of the cool, refreshing water of hope. In a crowd of critics and cynics, Matt Brown is a Barnabas to us, encouraging our hearts; he's a Jonathan, strengthening our hand in God. Matt tells us not what is wrong with the church, but what is right. He helps us see what God is doing around the world, strengthens our faith, and encourages us to join in this Great Work. Read the book, take heart, and find a need to meet."

> —**Jon Bloom,** president of Desiring God, @Bloom_Jon

"When Matt wanted to raise funds for Syrian refugees, he contacted me because he knew I had ministry friends in the Middle East. We'd never met, but I quickly saw Matt's earnest desire to be part of God's transforming work throughout the world. Let Matt's passion and vision inspire you to find your place in God's global story."

> —**Lynne Hybels,** Advocate for Global Engagement, Willow Creek Community Church

"Matt Brown's book is inspirational! It encourages us to pay attention to what God is doing all over the world. It inspires us to get involved and to influence those around us for the sake of the Gospel."

—**Naghmeh Abedini,** wife of imprisoned pastor, Saeed Abedini

"In Matt Brown's unique style, *Awakening* gently and unapologetically taps you on the shoulder and invites you to pull back the curtain on the greatness of God's activity in the world around you. Before you know it, you're embracing your smallness, celebrating God's bigness, and thankful you haven't missed any more of the story than you already have. With a personal, heartfelt delivery, Matt Brown invites you to be an eyewitness to the inspirational power that only God could orchestrate in the lives of those next door, across the street, and around the world. *Awakening* is a gospel-driven, beautifully written reminder that you can be an active participant in God's great big story; a story best lived with your eyes wide open."

—**Jimmy Peña,** *New York Times* bestselling author and founder of PrayFit® Ministries, Inc.

"*Awakening* is an inspiring book that will leave you rethinking your relationship with God for the better. Matt takes a vibrant approach toward digging deeper and exploring the truth of Jesus."

—**Jarrid Wilson,** blogger, pastor at LifePoint Church, author of *Jesus Swagger*

AWAKENING

AWAKENING

// HOW GOD'S
NEXT GREAT MOVE
INSPIRES & INFLUENCES
OUR LIVES TODAY

MATT BROWN

LEAFWOOD
PUBLISHERS
an imprint of Abilene Christian University Press

AWAKENING

How God's Next Great Move Inspires and Influences Our Lives Today

LEAFWOOD
P U B L I S H E R S
an imprint of Abilene Christian University Press

Copyright © 2015 by Matt Brown

ISBN 978-0-89112-417-7
LCCN 2014045228

Scripture quotations, unless otherwise noted, are from The Holy Bible, New International Version®, NIV®. Copyright © 1973, 1978, 1984, 2011 by Biblica, Inc.® Used by permission. All rights reserved worldwide.

Scripture quotations marked AMP are from the Amplified® Bible, Copyright © 1954, 1958, 1962, 1964, 1965, 1987 by The Lockman Foundation. Used by permission.

Scripture quotations noted ESV are from the ESV® Bible (The Holy Bible, English Standard Version®) copyright © 2001 by Crossway, a publishing ministry of Good News Publishers.

Scripture quotations marked HCSB are taken from the Holman Christian Standard Bible®, Copyright © 1999, 2000, 2002, 2003, 2009 by Holman Bible Publishers. Used by permission. Holman Christian Standard Bible®, Holman CSB®, and HCSB® are federally registered trademarks of Holman Bible Publishers.

Scripture quotations noted *The Message* taken from *The Message*. Copyright 1993, 1994, 1995, 1996, 2000, 2001, 2002. Used by permission of NavPress Publishing Group.

Scripture quotations noted NASB are taken from the New American Standard Bible® Copyright © 1960, 1962, 1963, 1968, 1971, 1972, 1973, 1975, 1977, 1995 by The Lockman Foundation. Used by permission.

Scriptures noted NKJV are taken from the New King James Version® Copyright © 1982 by Thomas Nelson. Used by permission. All rights reserved.

Scripture quotations noted NLT are taken from the New Living Translation, Copyright ©1996, 2004, 2007 by Tyndale House Foundation. Used by permission of Tyndale House Publishers, Inc., Carol Stream, IL 60188. All rights reserved.

Scripture quotations noted NRSV are taken from the New Revised Standard Version Bible, copyright © 1989, the Division of Christian Education of the National Council of the Churches of Christ in the United States of America. Used by permission. All rights reserved.

Scripture quotations noted TLB are taken from The Living Bible copyright © 1971 by Tyndale House Foundation. Used by permission of Tyndale House Publishers Inc., Carol Stream, IL 60188. All rights reserved.

Scripture quotations marked WNT are taken from the Weymouth New Testament.

Published in association with The Blythe Daniel Agency, Inc., PO Box 64197, Colorado Springs, CO 80962.

LIBRARY OF CONGRESS CATALOGING-IN-PUBLICATION DATA
Brown, Matt, 1983-
  Awakening : how God's next great move inspires and influences our lives today / Matt Brown.
     pages cm
  Includes bibliographical references and index.
  ISBN 978-0-89112-417-7 (alk-paper)
  1. Church history--20th century. 2. Church history--21st century. 3. God (Christianity) I. Title.
  BR479.B74 2015
  270.8'3--dc23

                                                                        2014045228

Cover design by Thinkpen Design, LLC | Interior text design by Sandy Armstrong, Strong Design

Leafwood Publishers is an imprint of Abilene Christian University Press
ACU Box 29138, Abilene, Texas 79699
1-877-816-4455 | www.leafwoodpublishers.com

                    15 16 17 18 19 20 / 7 6 5 4 3 2 1

CONTENTS

FORTY-KNOT WINDS AND WAKING UP TO GOD'S WORKING

There, in the midst of the ocean, I am overcome with a feeling of smallness. I realize how insignificant I am in the midst of the surging, awe-inspiring waves.

—**Alex Thomson,** solo around-the-world yacht racer

My wife, Michelle, and I experienced one of the most fascinating stories a month ago. We were in San Francisco, overlooking the beautiful bay during the America's Cup yacht races funded by billionaire Oracle founder Larry Ellison. We happened to be in town with a book publisher to see the work of a Chinese immigrant who had spent the past twenty-nine years working in the toughest area of the city. We even saw where Francis Chan had spent the past several years in an area known as the Tenderloin, with more than six thousand homeless in a single city street block.

It was staggering going from all that poverty to all this wealth just a few dozen blocks away. Massive yachts stood like expensive cars displayed for visitors to see. We watched a yacht owner sipping a drink on his deck as a dozen passersby stood gawking at his boat. Meanwhile, a handful of young guys scrubbed and cleaned various parts of the deck. *Must be an interesting life traveling around the world with eccentric businessmen and women on their vacation time*, I thought to myself. There are whole worlds we know nothing about, and yet people are the same in every culture. Some have great wealth. Others have great need. All need a Savior.

Large open areas were abundant throughout the veranda near the races, and Michelle and I plopped down on large red beanbags on the lawn in front of big TV screens. They were showing parts of yesterday's race mixed with promotional spots and a list of upcoming events. One of the stories was about Alex Thomson, who had sailed nonstop around the world multiple times. To give some perspective, three thousand people have climbed Mount Everest and five hundred people have been to space, but less than one hundred people have sailed solo nonstop around the world.

Everything about this race is not only rare, but also fascinating. When I was scouring recent interviews, I saw Alex mention that during the Vendée Globe, an eighty-day solo race around the world, nearly 50 percent of the racers don't finish the race. Racers cannot get more than twenty minutes of sleep at a time for the duration of the race because they are single-handedly racing such a large boat, which typically takes more than sixteen people to sail. Racers consume more than five thousand calories of freeze-dried food per day and endure a test of will, strength, and stamina that is unparalleled in the sports world. If the boat capsized out in the frigid waters, escape would be virtually impossible . . . he would die.

Thomson had just completed the Vendée Globe, which takes place every four years. It was his third try; the first two attempts he didn't finish. "You know when you're out there on your own in the Southern Ocean, where you're going to spend five weeks in wind chill factors of minus 20, and there's no one to help you . . . your brain is telling you you're going to die and you've got to learn to control that emotion. You've got to be able to sleep, you've got to be able to eat, you've got to be able to do your jobs and sail the boat. That takes some mental strength, also mental instability," Thomson told CNN.[1]

There, on the giant screens in San Francisco Bay, Thomson shared in the America's Cup video that when he's out in the middle of the ocean all by himself, as the waves pound on every side, *he is overcome with a feeling of smallness. He realizes how insignificant he is in the midst of the surging, awe-inspiring waves.*

This is exactly what happens when we leave the "local shores" of our own churches and denominations and branch out to see how God is moving around the world. There are incredible stories happening in Christianity all over the world today. They do not often make national news, but they are happening, and we would be greatly encouraged if we knew of them. All of a sudden, we wouldn't feel so discouraged, insignificant, or isolated in our faith. We are part of a much bigger movement: a great movement of God that depends on our role in it, just like Thomson's role in completing his race.

Most of the believers I've met at churches from many denominations across the country are unaware of how Christianity is flourishing around the world—and even down the street from where they live. They perceive the status of the global Christian faith through the microscopic lens of their local church, churches they may have heard of in their city, or what little they know of their denomination. This lack of knowledge and understanding of God's constant activity can lead to many problems in a believer's life—not just an unawareness of what God is doing, but a lack of understanding about our place in a much bigger story.

Whenever I've shared even a handful of stories with the hundreds of churches I've spoken for, believers are visibly encouraged by any crumb I give them in this wider perspective on the Christian world. It's easy to see why. With all that is going on in the world—political instability, persecution of Christians, tragedies, and wars—we need encouragement that God is at work all around us.

I will share with you how God is moving around the world in ways unprecedented in history and ask you to reflect on how being a part of this larger story affects your own story. I pray God uses these stories to awaken you to what I believe is part of the next Great Awakening. Are we ready for it? How can we begin to live with our eyes and ears more attuned to what other Christians are experiencing from God? How can those stories inspire us to reach for greater things from God?

The three sections in this book showcase the following three aims and some of the most fascinating stories taking place in Christianity today.

The first section is **Live Awake**. I want to call you to live awakened to the undercurrents of how God is moving on earth today. We all hope to live awake in our lives. We all have a fear of missing out. It's why we set reminders in our phones, so we don't miss a meeting or a game. But more importantly, we should fear missing out on what God is doing, and this can easily be the case if we don't make his kingdom and purposes a priority in our lives. We all desire to be involved in purposes much, much bigger than ourselves, yet we don't often know how to get there or set aside the time to do it. I want to invite you into God's bigger story. I want to help you see that you are already a part of something God is doing that is so much bigger than you are. As you see what God is capable of, I want to call you to greater things God has in store for you. *There is more for us, but we need to be awakened to it.*

In Section Two, we want to **Live Inspired**. We all want to live for something that takes us beyond ourselves that will matter eternally rather than just filling a role or occupying a space and not making a difference in our world for Christ. In order to discover our own purpose, we need to hear about God moving in other people's purposes. When we hear what God has done with others, it inspires us and expands our hearts with greater faith, vision, and purpose.

Scripture tells us we overcome by the blood of Jesus's finished work on the cross and by the word of our testimony. The power of testimony, or the power of a God-story, has been proven over and over again: a young person reads a biography of a missionary and it changes the trajectory of his or her life. *Hearing testimonies, or the stories of God moving in the lives of others, has a way of transforming our own lives like nothing else can.* We are missing out on not only the body of Christ globally, but also on how these stories of God moving could affect us personally if we just take time to listen to them. I am what I am today because of countless God-stories I have heard and experienced, and my life has taken a different route because of them. And I am just one of many who repurposed their lives after they heard about the plan God had for them and as they experienced how God moved in another person's life and purpose. These testimonies can be a source of bottomless inspiration for us if we take time to listen.

The third and final section is **Live Influential**. Carl F. Henry said, "The early Christians did not exclaim, 'What has the world come to?' Rather they proclaimed, 'Look what has come to the world!'"

We lose influence when we spend all our time preaching against the bad in culture. We gain influence when we preach about the good we have in Christ. No one really wants to hear about the religious differences or denominational feuds taking place in our churches today. It's exactly what nonbelievers point to and say, "Well, if they can't agree on what it takes to be a 'Christian,' then I certainly don't want to get mixed up in their issues."

Think for a moment about books, media, and examples of Christians fighting other Christians over theological differences. This isn't what we are to focus on. We are called to focus on Christ and what God is doing and saying to us. The Bible clearly says to focus on what is true, lovely, noble, and of good report.

To be sure, the early Christians challenged problems in the church, but their main message to those outside the church was, "The gospel is growing and bearing fruit all over the world." They didn't spend all their time focusing on who was right and who was wrong. They weren't trying to build a successful organization—they simply couldn't hold in all they had seen Jesus do and teach, or stories about all the lives he had changed for the better. They were part of a bigger movement—and so are we.

Christians are steadily losing influence in American culture, and I believe it is because we've become too busy preaching against things. We are too quick to point out when everyone else is making wrong choices or doing things we don't agree with. If we get back to the goodness, hope, joy, and love in the gospel, and how God is using his gospel in the lives of people all around us, we will retrieve a powerful antidote for the deepest needs of our culture. And we will be able to administer it with influence.

I'm not writing to tell you to "look what the world has come to." I want to open your eyes to "what has come to the world" in Christ and his greater story in his church. I want you to get lost in your own smallness and insignificance in the great movements of God all over the world, even as Alex Thomson sensed his smallness in the surging waves of the Southern Ocean. I believe that in this feeling of your own insignificance, you will actually lay hold of a greater sense of significance than you've ever known. But it will be based on God's greater story and bigger purpose, not on your own story.

Book Study Guide

Throughout this book, I'm going to ask you some personal questions. There is also a thirty-day challenge that I ask you to consider joining by simply going to my website and being part of a larger movement. Each challenge will take you through some practical things you can do to join God's larger story. What we're going to ask you to do will stretch you and expand your vision. I believe it will serve to point you in the right direction to make the most of your days and to look at what has come to us in this next movement of God happening right before our eyes. Will you join us?

Notes

[1]John Berman, "Sailing solo around the world," *CNN*, July 19, 2012, accessed October 24, 2014, http://earlystart.blogs.cnn.com/2012/07/19/sailing-solo-around-the-world-john-berman-talks-with-alex-thomson/.

Section One

LIVE AWAKE

Chapter One

NOTHING IMPORTANT HAPPENED TODAY

In the middle of our trouble and hard times here,
just knowing how you're doing keeps us going.
Knowing that your faith is alive keeps us alive.
—1 Thessalonians 3:8 *The Message*

On July 4, 1776, an unseasonably mild midsummer day in the typically hot and humid Philadelphia, the United States Declaration of Independence was finalized and adopted by fifty-six men, and was soon signed and distributed throughout the colonies. John Adams had convinced the Continental Congress, then at war with Great Britain, to allow the young Thomas Jefferson to compose the initial document formally explaining their choice to declare independence from Great Britain.

Also on that day, across the Atlantic Ocean, legend has it that King George III of England wrote in his diary: "Nothing important happened today."

Nothing important happened?!

This was perhaps one of the greatest understatements in world history. On that day, American rebels forged the Declaration of Independence, and although it took seven more years until the Americans fully achieved independence from

England, the writing of the Declaration was the beginning of the end of England's reign over America.

The king assumed nothing important had taken place on that day because he hadn't heard of it yet.[1] He didn't live in the day and age of tweets and texts and camera phones and search engines. His was a day of smoke signals.

It is my fear for the Western church today that, on the coattails of King George III, we make generalizations and assumptions about the fate of our Christian faith in this day and age and end up being wrong about what we think, or even say, to others in passing.

Christianity is thriving around the world today. There is a sense of revival on many fronts, but most of us haven't heard of it yet, and so we write on the subconscious journal in the recesses of our minds: "Nothing important is happening today." And we ask ourselves: *Is this all there is?* It is as if we think we have a cap on what God is doing around the world today.

But you and I have the chance to be a part of something really great. It's happening all over the world and we don't want to miss it. Remember how I asked you to get lost in the sense of the smallness of your own efforts and reach for, grab hold of, the greatness of our God? Do you have any idea what it could look like if we really did this out of our genuine desire to love God as he loves us? Mind-boggling, isn't it?

Trying to Get a Handle on Statistics We Cannot Truly Grasp

As my wife and I have been driving the highways of the Twin Cities over the past few months, I have been making mental notes on the many companies located along the sprawling metropolis of Minneapolis and Saint Paul. There are thousands of massive office buildings that bring in billions of dollars, and I have never heard of most of these businesses. I don't know what they do, but each one of them has a story.

And this is just one small region compared to the surrounding states and nearby metropolitan areas. The United States is just one small region in the vast expanse of the world economy and population centers. Buenos Aires, the capital city of the nation of Argentina, for example, is a region filled with European immigrants merged with the Spanish-speaking world. It is quite a delightful place to visit. Surprisingly, their capital city is four times the size of New York City, the largest metropolitan area in the United States. The same could be said of many other cities around the world. We rarely think about the impact of other people, their businesses, and their stories because we are so focused on our own.

In a similar way, the Christian church around the world—the sum of countless local churches across the earth today—is so much bigger and more impactful than we can grasp with our human intellect or sum up with our pithy statements and negative generalizations. We need to be awakened to the vastness of God and the church. There are so many more good things happening than we can wrap our minds around, and this reality should excite and invigorate us and our faith. The great works of God happening around the globe are exactly what inspired the awe of the disciples as they watched Jesus at work. We have the opportunity to be part of a life-changing season in history.

At this stage in history, the church has grown into many beautiful and powerful variations of practicing faith and represents billions of individuals and families and backgrounds and stories. And that's worth far more, eternally, than the sum total of a person's net worth. The sense of longing for more, looking for more, has been placed in our hearts from the beginning of time by the One who created us and longs to see us move in his direction. Let's focus on that thought for a minute.

From One in Three Million to One in Three

Consider for a moment where we've come from. At first glance, Christ wrote no books, established no government-recognized organizations, and posted no tweets. Instead, he taught many large crowds and poured his life into a few close followers.

The first followers of Christ continued to spread his message even after he left the earth, and his movement has grown into billions of followers. Think about that! What other religion can say its leader came to earth and was fully man (not a king enthroned with regality), was crucified and rose again, and before leaving the earth, charged followers who would believe in him (not a forced belief but of their own choosing) to give everything to share his gospel with others? Amazing!

Church history tells us the apostles divided up the known world for evangelism, and each began to travel to the ends of the earth, preaching this exclusive gospel of trusting in Jesus. One of the terms coined by Christ's earliest followers was the "Door of Jesus," which referred to Jesus as the one way to the one true God. They trumpeted this exclusive message in their day and age, when historians estimate that only one in three million people had ever heard the name of Jesus Christ.

There are Christians today who still give everything to bring this gospel to others, but times have changed. We typically think of this happening in "other countries," and many of us wouldn't dare share the gospel with our next-door neighbors. Would they be offended and avoid us, or even talk to others about their preachy neighbors? Surprisingly, today one in three people you run into on the street claims adherence to and faith in Jesus Christ. Did you know that?

One of our greatest challenges in this day and age is not whether something is happening with Christianity—it's that amazing works are happening, and we never hear about them, so we never plug into them.

Sure, we've now got social networks, camera phones, and multiple forms of messaging, and it's easier to share something than ever before in history. We are a long way from smoke signals, and *yet the majority of Christians remain in the dark about the amazing ways God is moving around the world, and stay in the dark when it comes to sharing Christ with others.* Why is this? Why don't we take greater interest in talking about what God is up to rather than what we are up to? If we did, it could awaken us to our life's purpose and inspire us in our life's direction. We spend a lot of time on a lot of things that don't have as much significant meaning as the gospel. But the gospel at work in people's lives? It is not just a Sunday event; it is a daily treasure.

A Quick Test

I think one of the things we face is oversaturation with all of the digital tools we have today, and we can get lost in them. Despite all the help they can give, there are some things you cannot find on search engines—including the answer to most of the following questions about the status of Christianity today and how big the movement of God really is globally.

1. Where is the largest church building in the world, and how many people does it seat?
2. Where is the largest church numerically in the world, and how big is it?
3. Who has preached the gospel in person to more people than anyone in human history?
4. What is the largest ministry staff in church history for an individual ministry (not denominational)?

The answer to number one is that while there are many gorgeous, massive cathedrals around the world, the largest church building in the world is rather new (built within the last century), in Nigeria, Africa, and seats nearly fifty thousand people for a single service.

The answer to number two is surprisingly in Nigeria as well, although it is not the same church as the largest church building. For many years, it was a church in Seoul, South Korea, called Yoiddo Full Gospel Church, a small-group-based church that has close to one million weekly attendees. A well-known church leader shared with me recently about another congregation in Nigeria with close to two million weekly attendees. The local church, he shared, holds a monthly prayer meeting out in the open field that draws as many as eight million Africans crying out for a move of God on the earth today. For years, the Western church has proclaimed the need for missionaries and pointed to Africa. Now, increasingly, it seems Africa is sending missionaries to the Western world.

The answer to number three is a preacher who has spent his life in Africa. A German-born missionary by the name of Reinhard Bonnke leads an organization known as Christ for All Nations that has communicated the gospel to more people than any other in human history. Billy Graham's largest crusade was in South Korea in 1979, and he preached in person to more than one million people in a single service. Reinhard Bonnke's largest crusades have been held in Africa, and he preached to several million on a dusty field in Nigeria in 2001, and more than one million people dedicated their lives to Jesus Christ in a single service! Surprisingly, many Westerners are unaware of Bonnke. We often look for the "big names" in Christianity but don't even recognize the men and women God is using that we have right in front of us.

The largest ministry team in church history was that of a minister by the name of Vincent Ferrer, whom the Catholic church has since named a saint. He ministered in the fifteenth century, around the same time as Martin Luther, and he had as many as ten thousand people on his ministry team who traveled with him across Europe on foot as they spread the gospel.

Most of these encouraging facts, along with a multitude of others, are *unknown by the average Christian today*. They are missed. But as you'll see, we humans tend to miss many big things, in many areas of society.

Isn't it staggering to read about the vast number of people who are hearing the gospel and, even more so, the courage of those who are bringing it? These kinds of stories could impact and inspire you and me to the greater things God has for us. Hearing about these people should stir our hearts and move us into action. But we often miss our moments. What can we do in our own neighborhoods? Some churches are effectively bringing in those who need to hear the gospel. But some are not as effective in this area, and many Christians don't attend church at all. What can you do to show the life of Christ that is in you to others? We need to be willing to take what we know to be true and share it with those who don't yet know it. We want to awaken them to the same life that we have because of Christ.

Why This Is Personal and Why This Book Matters

I don't know what kind of church you grew up in, but I do think that how we are raised has a lot to do with the lens through which we view the church and the world today.

To show where the rubber meets the road for many Christians today, I will start with my story. I grew up for the first few decades of my life in a small church near the Twin Cities. My experience was similar to the majority of American Christians today. As badly as we all want to be on the fastest-growing-churches-in-America list, the reality is that there are only a handful of slots for those, and 90 percent of Americans attend small churches. The average size of a Protestant church in America is just 124 people.

My upbringing happened to be in a small church of about 100 to 150 believers on any given weekend, and had a strong family feel. We fit the description of the average Protestant church to a T. Throughout the first several decades of my life, the church slowly declined numerically. I think the lack of excitement in my church growing up is why I'm such an overeager seeker of God's movement around the world today. But it's not just about numbers in churches; it's about so much more. When you're raised in a small church (and most of us are), you don't know a whole lot about other movements and the great activity of God around the world. I never get tired of hearing stories of how God is at work in other places. To me, it's just so encouraging to find fellow followers of Christ; their stories impact how and what I do and the way I think.

My wife Michelle grew up in a very different story . . . one you might expect to read about in church history books or something. Her grandpa immigrated with his young family from Canada, and after a stint and some unexpected disappointment in Chillicothe, a small town in northern Missouri, he ended up as the pastor of a new church near the city of Minneapolis. Rev. G. Mark Denyes pastored that church for nearly forty-five years, and the church grew from several families meeting in a basement of a home into one of the largest churches in the nation. He led the church through seven building programs, and it now features a 3,100-seat auditorium.

With this miraculous church growth, Michelle's experience in youth group was very different from mine.

My youth group experience mostly consisted of a small group of no more than a dozen, which was always tough during worship since half of us were in the worship band. Maybe you know what I'm talking about because this mirrors your own experience. Most of the young people I grew up with are now doing ministry all over the world, but I can't say we wouldn't have been excited to see more numerical growth during those years, so we wouldn't feel like we were small and going it alone. Even if we didn't see growth ourselves, maybe someone could've shared about the great works God was doing in other places. It would have provided that needed inspiration and momentum for us.

Michelle's youth group in the 1990s consisted of upwards of a thousand students. The weekly youth service, the small groups, and the leadership were growing and firing on all cylinders. Her youth pastor at that time, Nate Ruch, led the youth leaders and students with godly, passionate leadership, and God was active in their church community in powerful ways. I once heard Nate share a story about how other youth pastors would come up to him and ask questions such as, "Isn't it great to have such a big youth ministry?" His response to these comments was: "The devil's got the biggest youth ministry in town, and we've got work to do." It's that kind of statement that helps us realize our perspective can change everything.

My wife's church, *Emmanuel*, was literally down the highway from mine, and I still remember the first time I visited there in my late teens. I was in awe of the size of the sanctuary and the enthusiasm of the people there. It was quite remarkable for a young man from a small church. I think sometimes we take for granted that we have seen big churches or conferences, not realizing that our kids or friends or family have not had the opportunity to experience the larger number of worshippers and fellow Christ-followers with us. Some Christians feel isolated and part of something small. But it is a massive movement if we will but stop and recognize it.

Maybe this is one reason summer camp is so influential in young people's lives. They realize the kingdom of God is a lot bigger than they had realized. But it's not enough to see it for ourselves; we need to tell others about these experiences and get them in places to experience movements like this as well. We probably don't realize how much our hearts depend on good news and how we need to know that we are part of something much bigger than our own stories every day. We need to live awake to the realities around us.

There are six main reasons this book matters for your walk of faith and mine.

The majority of American Christians today have tunnel vision. Megachurches account for about 10 percent of all church attendance in America, leaving 90 percent of church attendees with a more limited perspective on the church at large. Because the average size of a Protestant church in America is 124 people, many Christians have never been in a church gathering larger than a few hundred people. Growing up in a small church, I know all about tunnel vision and the feeling that church is less-than-exciting and anything-but-glorious. Access to outside perspectives of a "thriving and flourishing faith" is minimal for most of us.

Beyond church attendees, there is a significant majority of the American population that claims adherence to faith in Christ but does not attend church. Statisticians estimate that 20 to 40 percent of Americans attend church regularly, meaning there are potentially an additional 60 percent of American believers with little to no church attendance, and even greater tunnel vision than the 90 percent of American Christians in small churches. Their experience of church may be limited to a TV preacher, a radio program, a Christian book, or content from Christian websites and social media.

Honestly, even for those Christians in thriving churches, many are oblivious to what God is doing around the world, beyond their own church or a few churches in their area, and their little knowledge of their denomination. Even most fully engaged followers of Christ are missing out on the bigger picture that God is at work in unprecedented ways in our generation. And it's not just in handfuls. A large part of the population is in this category.

I once took one of my close friends to a conference that happened to be in town. I picked him up, and we drove over to the conference, which was at a local church near his house. I asked him how much he knew about the church we were going to visit—Eagle Brook Church, a sizable Baptist church with several locations across the Twin Cities. I assumed everyone had heard of this church because of its magnitude. To my great surprise, Luke had not.

Luke is a very serious follower of Christ. He is involved in various ministries and has been greatly used by God to reach many people with the gospel. This church was in his city, down the street from his house, and he hadn't heard of it. It's not Luke's fault—it's simply a fact: most Christians, even the serious ones, don't know what God is doing around them. To paint the picture a bit more, Eagle Brook is actually the largest church in a five-state region, with seventeen thousand weekly attendees and twenty-seven thousand attendees over Easter weekend that year! Imagine having that kind of presence, but those around you not even knowing about it. This is the case for many believers, in many areas of our country.

The vast majority of believers today are in the dark: completely unaware of exciting things taking place at churches down the street, let alone around the world. As a result, many Christians today walk around discouraged, fearful, and anxious about the future of our faith. It doesn't have to be this way. In fact, it can't if we're going to survive with a united front as believers.

There is great power in testimony.

It's no secret in the press that American Christianity is on the decline. One report states that church attendance is shrinking, while another exclaims that young adults are leaving the church in droves. What these reports are not sharing is news about some of the exciting gatherings of the church happening in America, as well as the fact that Christianity is exploding all over the world.

In America today, we get enough bad news. We need good news, too, for our weary souls. Paul wrote the church in Thessalonica saying something quite similar: "In the middle of our trouble and hard times here, just knowing how you're doing keeps us going. Knowing that your faith is alive keeps us alive" (1 Thess. 3:8 *The Message*). As believers, we know that there is power in testimony. Hearing about good works that God is doing with other people will empower and elevate our own efforts for Christ. The only problem is that we don't get enough reports of what God is doing with others.

Not everything newsworthy makes the news.

In 2013, one-half million people, including many millennials, marched on Washington, DC, in protest against abortion. The news media all but ignored this staggering statement and chose to spend their time on several small marches against gun control.

There's no way to fully understand the behemoth that is the American news media and their news cycle, but the simple fact is that not everything newsworthy makes the news. Especially when it comes to stories important to many American believers. It is part of the challenge we face as we seek to spread the Good News. Our news is considered politically incorrect or too biased for the media. I'm not sure if there will ever be change within the media circles, but I do know we are called to share the gospel and let God worry about the results. We can't depend on the media to be our source of news for what God is doing on earth today.

God is pictured too small.

There is a question that's been haunting me lately: What if the apostles preached the way many Christian leaders do today?

What if the apostles had shared negative statistics about how the faith is being trampled, and believers are dwindling, and culture is going to hell in a handbasket? Would that negative kind of message have inspired early Christians to trust in Christ? Probably not.

Stories of God's work on earth give practical testimony to the greatness of God. *Stories of God intervening take our theology and belief about him out of the stuffy closet of inexperience and into the real world where we need God to be most.* Hearing how God is moving in real people's stories gives us a larger picture of God, and how much he is able to move and desires to move in our lives today.

We need each other.

The Lausanne Movement declared during their Cape Town 2010 gathering: "A divided Church has no message for a divided world. Our failure to live in reconciled unity is a major obstacle to authenticity and effectiveness."[2]

Unfortunately, the vast majority of believers in America today are too splintered and divided to get news of what is taking place in other churches, denominations, and movements.

The Bible calls us all the body of Christ and expresses our great need for each other. To discard some "parts" or movements is not to function at full capacity. We need each other. *We need to hear more about each other all across the earth. It will greatly bless and increase our faith if we do.* This is what calls us to action. When we hear what other people are doing, we also are more encouraged to get involved and help each other where there are needs rather than just feeling like an island without being very effective in our own ministry.

Some Christians seem to think that intensity about non-essentials (the parts of theology not core to the gospel) is more important than unity with other believers. They have missed the heart of God. Jesus prayed intensely that we would come together as one and see each other as important and essential to the greater whole.

We need inspiration for our own efforts.

Hearing how God is moving in other places encourages and inspires our faith for what God wants to do in our own corner of the world.

A ministry in the Minneapolis region recently posted online: "The Bible isn't just a record of what God's done, it's a reminder of what God wants to do."[3] Likewise, when we hear about God moving in another part of the world, we are encouraged to seek this same blessing for our own community. Isn't it true for other areas of your life? When you hear that your friend is joining a program that will help him or her network for business and increase his or her presence, and you hear all the ways it has helped them, aren't you also drawn to be a part? No one wants to be left without the advantage of being part of a network. In the same way, we need to encourage and inspire others in our "network" of fellow believers, trying to point people to the only hope and answer we have in a world of hurt and disappointment: Jesus Christ.

The purpose of this book is to share many real-world examples and express the importance of being aware of God's move in the world. I hope you will be willing to do something in your own way, in your own city, that effectively continues to move forward what God has put in you to do with him. My prayer is that you, your family, your friends, and your church will be deeply encouraged and inspired in your faith and will in turn spur new movements of faith in your own area.

Go to www.thinke.org for Challenge #1.

To Think About

1. What examples are you aware of that point to individuals or groups of people being transformed by the gospel?

2. What would it look like in your own life if you truly believed that you have an impact on the great movement of God happening right now?

3. What will you purpose to do this week in your neighborhood, city or town, workplace, or church that reflects "being awake" to the call to recognize what God is doing around us?

4. Do you believe that God is still moving around the world today, and if so, how does that change your day-to-day living?

Notes

[1] NPR claims after sharing this story that they discovered it is merely legend. (Source: www.npr.org/templates/story/story.php?storyId=11703583). According to Arnold Hunt, curator of historical manuscripts at the British Library, King George III never kept a journal. He claims the quote is a variation of another well-known story from the French revolution. On July 14, 1789—the date of the storming of the Bastille—Louis XVI of France wrote in his diary "rien" (nothing). Hunt says Louis was referring to a hunting trip where he came back empty-handed. However, it seems possible Hunt would bury this piece of embarrassing history, since he is the primary one who could possibly confirm this story, and it is also ironic that he attributed the folklore to the French instead. We may never be able to confirm the truth.

[2] "A Confession of Faith and a Call to Action: Partnering in the body of Christ for unity in mission," *The Lausanne Movement,* 2011, accessed October 24, 2014, http://www.lausanne.org/content/ctc/ctcommitment-2#p2-5.

[3] Campus Movement, September 5, 2012, accessed October 24, 2014, https://twitter.com/CampusMovement/status/243508721198718976.

Chapter Two

THE POWER AND GLORY OF STORY

Keep your eyes open for God, watch for his works;
be alert for signs of his presence.

—Psalm 105:5 *The Message*

A s I write these words, I am perched on the eighth floor of a building overlooking the beautiful mountains and buildings of San Pedro Sula, Honduras. This beautiful, green nation in Central America, stacked between Guatemala and El Salvador, is known for having the most homicides per capita of any other in the world. My friends Dominic and Lindsay, on the cusp of their thirties, have been praying and planning for years, and in the past week, thousands of young Americans, mostly in their twenties, have converged on the nation to live out and speak the gospel.

Their organization specializes in taking believers on trips around the world for short periods of time, known as short-term missions. Previously, they had never taken a team larger than several hundred, but this particular week, the largest foreign mission team in the world came together to blitz the nation with the love and hope of Jesus Christ. Together, alongside thousands of Hondurans, they preached the gospel openly in every single school in the nation. Hundreds of thousands of dollars of medical supplies were shipped in on eighteen freights, and thousands of people were treated for free who could not afford care on their own.

Two days ago, we experienced a strong sense of God's presence for many hours as twenty-two thousand pastors and leaders gathered to pray for the divine blessing of God on their country in San Pedro Sula and Tegucigalpa. They put their faith together to pray and believe that God would bring change that only he could bring.

Yesterday, during what was called "1 Nation 1 Day," more than one million people attended across the nation in eighteen stadiums, in all eighteen regions of the country. All six major networks across the nation aired the historic gathering, and President Lobo himself was present and promoting the gathering. I sat in the green room as he, along with the team, called the nation to a "new Honduras" of peace, goodwill, and trust in God.

Ironically (you can't make this stuff up), I have encountered multiple short-term mission teams from various denominational backgrounds in my few short days here that knew nothing about the nation-changing event that was taking place. This, even though it was broadcast on every major TV network, aired on virtually every radio station, and splashed on the front page of every major newspaper. *God was doing something historic right under their noses, and they didn't even know it until I told them.*

It reminds me of the apostle Paul running into the dozen disciples on the road to Ephesus in Acts 19. Their response to his question was: "We have not even heard that there is a Holy Spirit" (Acts 19:2b). Imagine, the Spirit has been poured out, and the church is thriving and growing by leaps and bounds—something nation-changing—yet until these men were filled in by Paul, they were in the dark about the amazing outpouring of God's Spirit.

Before 1 Nation 1 Day, the financial capital of Honduras, San Pedro Sula, had been coined "The World's Murder Capital," with a reported twenty homicides every single day. It's probably good that I didn't realize this before I left on the trip, since I was staying in that city. In the year since the event, Francisco Guerrera, a member of the national security council of Honduras, reported the number of homicides has dropped from twenty murders per day to just six—a decline of approximately 75 percent. That is the power of the gospel.

Scripture promised this kind of blessing for this kind of effort: "Blessed is the nation whose God is the LORD, the people he chose for his inheritance" (Ps. 33:12). "When the godly are in authority, the people rejoice. But when the wicked are in power, they groan" (Prov. 29:2 NLT).

Collecting Stories of God at Work

There is a reason the Bible is filled with stories of God's mercy at work in people's lives, and not just commandments. God's goodness and activity in our lives is the fuel for our obedience to him. Our work for him is always in response to his work on our behalf. Stories of God at work are the sinew and substance out of which we can build our lives of obedience to God. We can see ourselves in the stories of Samson, David, and Samuel, and we can see ourselves in the lives of great men and women of God we read about who gave their lives for missions or pastored the same church for fifty years. These kinds of stories of God's faithfulness in the lives of others inspire us and fill us with hope.

If God does something dramatic in your family—say, for instance, he turns around the life of one of your uncles, setting him free from a life of addiction and abuse—that story will be powerful and transformative for the rest of your family only if you continue to pass it on. Now suppose a cousin begins to run with the wrong crowd and becomes open to trying drugs. If the story of your uncle's deliverance is not expressed to her, she will not have that ground on which to base her decision to abstain and protect herself.

It is the same with the stories of God moving in a church, a community, or a life. Nothing will inspire us and continue to feed us as much as hearing the stories of God's grace replayed just when we need them most. We all need an arsenal of stories of how God turned situations around, and moved just in time, so we can build our lives on the reality of his purposes on earth. This causes us to live awake to his greater purposes for our lives. Psalm 111:2 calls to us this life of story collecting: "How amazing are the deeds of the LORD! All who delight in him should ponder them" (NLT).

For many years, I've been a story collector of God's activity on earth. As I do this, it only increases my desire to know more. Psalm 105:5 speaks to me: "Keep your eyes open for GOD, watch for his works; be alert for signs of his presence" (*The Message*). Do you regularly watch for God-at-work stories, too? Maybe you already do, and this book will help you continue on this incredible adventure. Wherever you are, there are more stories to be uncovered and rediscovered. I hope you will join me in this journey of being a story collector of God at work, and allow it to build you as a follower of Jesus throughout the rest of your life.

As you become a story collector, also become a storyteller—passionate to share God's loving works in practical ways with those you care about. Scripture calls to us: "Repeat them again and again to your children. Talk about them when you are at home and when you are on the road, when you are going to bed and when you are getting up. Tie them to your hands and wear them on your forehead as reminders. Write them on the door-posts of your house and on your gates" (Deut. 6:7–9 NLT). This biblical challenge tells us that our dream shouldn't simply be a house with a yard and a white picket fence, unless that white picket fence has God-stories featured on it. We should instead seek a house full of stories of God's promises and God's ways. This is the blessed life.

This pursuit started for me during a profound spiritual awakening that occurred in the community where I went to high school: something so significant, I don't think I will ever be the same.

Monday Night Jam

I grew up in a Christian home. Not a perfect home, but a quiet, simple kind of upbringing that revolved around church life. My parents were not pastors, but they served the Lord and the church with fervor and faithfulness. My dad was an elder at the local church we went to, and anytime the doors of the church were open, we were almost always there. But going to church is not enough to cause a child to go in the right direction. We need the activity of God in a tangible and practical way. In fact, one minute of God moving in a church is more effective in a young person's life than a thousand fire-and-brimstone sermons. We need more than truth. We need the Spirit. We need God to show up in practical ways that we can see with our eyes and feel with goose bumps.

Just such a moment occurred while I was still in public high school. I remember meeting Luke when he came to a concert we held at our church, which is almost an hour away from where he lived in Delano, Minnesota, a quiet, rural farming community. He had recently come to faith in Christ. It wasn't until many months later that I would hear his full story. Ed Kline, an evangelist within the Catholic church, had come into town and ministered a missions week at the local Catholic church in Delano. Luke and most of his family had an encounter of faith in Christ. Luke and several of the youth from the town were so deeply impacted by Ed's time in Delano that they started a small worship night where they would gather any student who wanted to come and simply sing modern worship songs for an hour or more.

Soon I heard about this worship night, dubbed Monday Night Jam, from excited students in the high school who knew me from leading the campus Bible club. I made my way over and had to see this gathering where I had heard more than sixty students gathered on a weeknight to sing and seek God. Even more amazing, no pastor had gathered the group. It was simply a bunch of students with such a hunger for God that they started it on their own.

Within a few months, I had joined the worship band for Monday Night Jam, and soon there was hardly room for anyone in the small Common Grounds Coffeehouse on River Street. Students would stand behind the counter where baristas normally worked and even in the back room where supplies were stocked. As if that wasn't enough, students would come in and have to leave because there was not room in the small one-room building for anyone else.

We had to pursue other options. We came up with a bold plan to ask the public high school principal if we could utilize the school auditorium for this weekly, student-led night of worship. Mr. Mays had come to faith in Christ several years before this, so he did his best to get the school board to agree to our plan. They said yes.

For the next several years, four to six hundred students gathered weekly to worship and seek God. My most significant memory from Monday Night Jam was that the presence of God was tangible and thick. Several times I had to miss the worship night to participate in school band or choir programs, and I can still remember walking over to the other parts of the building where the worship night was in progress—it felt as if I were walking into a wall of God's presence. The presence of God was so strong that many of the students would walk into the hallways and start crying under the encounter. On many weeks, students would come to faith in Christ without anyone even preaching the gospel. As we grew in understanding, we eventually started having short messages that would call people to put their faith in Christ. Other biblical miracles took place, and near the end of this time, our high school principal wrote us a very nice letter that shared that "for an entire year, zero disciplinary problems had taken place" in a public high school in America—in a day and age of school shootings.

This organic, student-led movement eclipsed even my local church in scope and impact, and yet it had none of the professional and political undergirding it takes to pull together most church bodies. Students from many denominations came together to lift up Christ and pursue God together. Church vans full of people hungry for God would come in from an hour away, sometimes up to several hours away, for an hour of worship because they heard about what God was doing in our midst.

It was from this experience that I began to see my faith with different eyes. Not only what God could do when students came together from across the state for dedicated time to seek him together, but also what God could do when students from even one community came together with a common hunger for God to move in their midst. Soon I would have more experiences, some of which are included in these pages to encourage you and to applaud the efforts you are making, and can continue to make, by stepping out on a limb to usher God into your community. It has far-reaching effects, and in the process, we are inspired to keep the faith we want others to grasp.

Every time I preach, and every time I talk to others about faith, I have a choice: *I can preach and talk about the negative statistics that so frequently find their way onto the news, or I can preach and talk about my personal experiences of God moving in amazing ways on earth today, and of the countless stories I have heard about God defying all the odds and using his people in all the corners of the world*. I would rather do the latter. And my guess is that people would rather hear the latter. It is my heartfelt prayer that you, too, will be encouraged to think and speak differently about the Christian faith as you prayerfully read through the rest of this book.

A Few Mind-Boggling Stories

I want to share just a few stories with you of what is happening around the world today and whet your appetite. I often feel like part teacher, part journalist as I share with others what I'm seeing in countries and ministries around the world. I want to awaken you to some of the stories taking place that have impressed my heart over the years.

Seoul, South Korea

We hear about North Korea in the news a lot nowadays, and it's never good. However, we hear less about South Korea. South

Korea has been experiencing spiritual revival for many decades. Billy Graham preached to the largest crowd of his life there in the 1970s with over a million people in attendance. Also, a pastor by the name of David Yonggi Cho, who was inspired by and strove to be "the next Billy Graham," prayed and worked to see what is now the largest-attended church in the world, with over eight hundred thousand weekly attendees in South Korea. The church is passionate and prayerful, not to mention it causes traffic jams every weekend. My late grandfather-in-law had the opportunity to meet and spend time with Pastor Cho many years ago when he came to Minneapolis to speak at a prayer conference. Can you fathom what it would be like to worship together with eight thousand people in one big church service? Let alone more than one hundred times that number—eight hundred thousand? The largest crowds John Wesley and George Whitefield preached to were about thirty thousand people. They would be astounded at what is happening today.

Nigeria, Africa

While many nations across Africa face great turmoil and unrest these days, over the past one hundred years, many have experienced nation-shaking revival like never before in all of history. Entire African nations have gone from a small minority of Christians to a vast majority of Christians in just a single generation. One evangelist has played a significant role in the African nation of Nigeria, where the nation has gone from 10 percent Christian to over 60 percent Christian in our lifetime. This is the nation that has the largest church building in the world mentioned in Chapter One. This is also a nation that contains what is recently the largest church congregation in the world, with more than two million members. This church

47

also holds a regular prayer meeting that has gathered as many as eight million Nigerians crying out to God to move on earth and come quickly. The first person I personally heard about this congregation from was author John Bevere, when Michelle and I spent time with him in Minneapolis in 2012. Since that time, I've spoken with several Nigerian-born Americans who have confirmed this story.

According to Wikipedia, Charles Spurgeon preached to ten million people over his lifetime. But this would have been mostly repeat church attendees week after week. His church at its peak had about ten thousand people, and Spurgeon did not travel regularly like the Wesleys or other itinerant ministers in church history.

Comparatively, one German-born missionary evangelist to Africa, Reinhard Bonnke, preached to more than ten million people in a single year. In fact, his ministry, Christ for All Nations, has seen more than fifty million people make decisions for Christ across Africa in the first decade of the twenty-first century. Can you imagine being in these crowds? There are videos online that show some of these mass outreaches. This is outreach on a scale never before seen in history.

Just to further emphasize how truly amazing this is, a good friend and minister from the Detroit area named Chris was at a national denominational conference in Orlando a few years back. He called me huffing and puffing, as he had walked by a booth sharing about the work of Christ for the Nations, and none other than Reinhard Bonnke himself was standing alone at his booth. Chris watched as pastors and leaders and congregants streamed by, no one stopping because they hadn't heard of Bonnke's work and didn't recognize him. He knew how much I liked Bonnke and cherished his work for the Lord.

I received his newsletters for years growing up and was always amazed and stirred as I unfolded the large pictures showing the crowds that had gathered to hear the gospel across the African continent. In fact, it may have been those newsletters that played a role in opening me up to God's activity at an early age. I have not seen many books or online articles about Bonnke and his work. He is charismatic, yet his presentations of the gospel are biblical and powerful, and you can sense the activity and work of God when you hear him speak. Now Bonnke has set up the ministry to pass to the next generation through a younger leader named Daniel Kolenda, and he continues his ministry, in large part, online through posting daily to over a million fans on Facebook.

Bogotá, Columbia

Recently, I got together with some childhood friends for a birthday party. One friend, Jordan, shared with me how he and the executive team from his church had been meeting with the Leadership Network, a movement near Dallas connecting larger churches with each other to learn and grow. The stories from those meetings alone are enough to fill any believer in America with solid hope. Jordan's large church near Minneapolis is an extremely young church, with 90 percent of those attending under the age of thirty-five and 80 percent people who were previously unchurched. Every weekend, thousands gather in several locations, and the atmosphere and energy is contagious.

Jordan shared a handful of other examples of churches adding new believers at a mind-boggling rate, including Church of the Highlands in Birmingham, Alabama, that added eight thousand new members over the past year. Most of these new members were not "transfer growth" from other churches, but people who had been previously unchurched. That's eight thousand new people at one church in one year! That sounds like the Book of Acts on the day of Pentecost several times over. Can you imagine what it would feel like if your church added eight thousand people in the next year?

Another church Jordan shared about is in Bogotá, Columbia, with nearly three hundred thousand church members. I interrupted him in the middle of his story because I already knew about the church. About a decade before, my older brother Jon, a youth pastor near Chicago, had traveled down to Bogotá for a conference at this church. Not only were there church leaders around the world learning from this congregation of more than a quarter million people, but my brother also had the opportunity to attend their weekly youth service, which meets in a soccer stadium with more than seventy thousand students who attend weekly.

Buenos Aires, Argentina

God has been actively at work in the nation of Argentina over the past half-century. In the 1950s in Argentina, the average evangelical church was seven people. Through some major prayer, the nation has turned to the gospel within our lifetime. Now evangelical churches of twenty, thirty, or even fifty thousand are not uncommon. One evangelist, Carlos Annacondia, whom Michelle and I have spent time with several times now, has led the nation in revival for several decades and has led millions of people to faith in Christ. He had been a businessman, and in his late forties, he heard the gospel and responded in faith to Christ. Within a few years, he began preaching the gospel open-air, with thousands and eventually millions who would respond in faith to Jesus Christ. One of the board members of our nonprofit, Think Eternity, is president of a Bible college in the city of Buenos Aires. His students have played a key role in facilitating and pastoring these new flocks of believers who are coming into the churches at an alarming rate. A common problem in many areas of the world, including Africa and South America, is that there are not enough well-trained pastors to care for the new believers coming in.

Michelle and I traveled to Argentina a decade ago to see what was taking place and to serve the churches there. What we experienced rivals any other area of the world we have visited. There is a pervasive sense of God's passionate movement among the believers there. They pray with a level of faith and trust in God's care and concern for them and their fellow neighbors that is staggering. You don't have to try to get them excited or stirred for the work of the Lord. They are collectively pursuing the transformation of their entire nation. It seems that every single church member is on the same page. What an incredible model this is of one church working toward the same mission.

When we traveled there in 2002, it was the first time we met Carlos Annacondia in person. The missionaries who picked us up at the airport shared that the well-known pastor we were to visit that evening happened to be out of town. My face dropped with discouragement until they shared that Annacondia just so happened to be preaching at the church our missions team was scheduled to attend that evening. He only preaches there once a year or so out of the multiple services they hold each week, and he just happened to be preaching on the one night we would ever attend in our lives.

This church, known as Rey del Reyes in the heart of Buenos Aires, had been running church services at a rate of fourteen per week, including seven on Sundays, for years to keep up with their people's hunger for God. We attended one of those seven Sunday services and stood in line to get into the church. Far more people packed into the church that Sunday evening than probably any fire code would allow in a U.S. church, and the service was off to a start in a language we did not know. But the presence of God transcends language barriers and nationalities. God's presence heals, restores, and transforms lives and relationships.

The speakers blared far more loudly than in the North American churches we had been to, and the worship team and leaders cried out to God over distorting microphones, asking God to come and touch people in a big way. As Annacondia got up to preach, he shared from Scripture, and with compassionate, tear-filled eyes, he pointed people to the historical Jesus whose power is still available today. As he prayed loudly over the crowd toward the end of his message, I watched in amazement, as it seemed the wave of God's presence appeared to be so powerful it almost knocked people over, especially some of the older women in the middle section next to where we were sitting. He rebuked the devil's work in the lives of those in attendance and proclaimed the Biblical promise of freedom over them, asking God to do a great work in their lives. It was unlike what you see in most churches in America, but very powerful and life-changing.

In some of the other services we participated in around the area, we continued to be amazed at the people of God in that nation. Across many denominations, there was a mutual hunger for God expressed in the way they worshipped, prayed, read Scripture together, and reached out to people on the streets. In one church we attended, the service lasted for seven hours. It seemed one service ran into the next. Our entire team was exhausted by the end of it all. Exhausted, but happy and excited about what the Lord was doing. That is the heartbeat of this book: to share this excitement with you and to encourage you in your walk with God.

Minneapolis, United States

God is moving in the United States, too. In the midst of the hopelessness many believers feel in the face of our culture that is redefining marriage, that is steadfast in its commitment to allow abortion, and that seems to be growing irritated with biblical Christianity, there are still many signs for great hope. We see God's concern and care for our nation, and we see believers who are concerned about the future of the church.

I have been an eyewitness to some incredible works God has done in the Minneapolis-Saint Paul region of the Midwest where we live. As much as I've been an active participant in what has taken place, I feel more like an awestruck bystander at the works only God could have accomplished.

Several years ago, a group of pastors in our region planned some special prayer services called Awaken. These leaders booked a young worship leader from the Kansas City area, Matt Gilman, to come up and lead us in prayer and worship for God to do a greater work in our communities. With little preparation and promotion, thousands of area believers came together over two nights in the northern and southern metro regions of the Twin Cities for hours of fervent prayer. It was a prayer meeting not for the faint of soul.

To my great excitement, one of the churches in the southern metro we visited happened to be the home church of the late Leonard Ravenhill, decades ago. Ravenhill happens to be one of my favorite authors and a beloved Christian author on revival and prayer. The church was standing-room-only before the prayer meeting even started, and the crowd continued to overflow into the halls throughout the evening. To our great surprise, his church members told us that this was the largest gathering they had experienced at the church in over seventy years—even since the time Ravenhill himself had attended. When was the last time your church had a prayer meeting that resulted in overflow attendance, traffic jams, and standing-room-only crowds? This is happening in many areas of the world today. I cannot help but think that Ravenhill would have been moved by the crowds and the atmosphere of prayer that evening.

A few years ago, I spent the better part of a year working full time for the Billy Graham Evangelistic Association toward an outreach called Rock the River, put on by Franklin Graham, bringing the gospel to the next generation in America. I was moved by their organization's emphasis on prayer and calling upon God to move in all of their work, as well as their incredible emphasis on follow-up and making disciples to the best of their ability. I've never seen another church or ministry focus more intently on these areas than they did.

This was an incredible opportunity for me personally, as I have sensed a growing impression from God to do outreach ministry similar to their work for more than a decade. I learned so much, but more than that, I saw God move mightily and in concrete ways in so many people's lives. In August of that year, prayer teams held on-site vigils twenty-four hours a day for more than a week at the outdoor field where the event was to be held. The day of the event, on Harriet Island Park in downtown Saint Paul, more than twenty-three thousand young people gathered to hear the preaching of the gospel. More than one hundred twelve thousand young people gathered in all of the four cities where the tour passed that summer.

This is more astounding when you consider that even American Idol, with all its promise of fame and fortune, has still not gathered a crowd that size in any of its auditions. Their largest auditions were in Washington, DC, with twenty-two thousand young people waiting in lines throughout the day to try out.

Still more astounding is the fact that none of the major newspapers in the Twin Cities wrote a front-page story about the Rock the River event, even though they were solicited. The front page of the music section in one major paper promoted a concert down the street in Saint Paul featuring some significant secular rock bands, but that gathering only drew six thousand young people. Even Beyoncé's concert in the Twin Cities only drew a crowd of thirteen thousand young people. This experience cemented into my spirit what can happen when the church comes together around the gospel for seasons of unified prayer and outreach.

In a Day and Age of Social Media

Some of the signs of spiritual awakening in the world today can be found on social media. Local pastors that you've probably never heard of have tens of thousands or even hundreds of thousands of real followers on social media.

The business magazine *Fast Company* reports, "Celebrities aren't the only ones who can claim royal status on Twitter."[1] Though he might not be Kim Kardashian, the Pope has already collected hundreds of thousands of followers for his Twitter account. It's not surprising that holy high rollers are drawn to the medium: religious leaders on average pull more weight per tweet, with one retweet for every five hundred followers. In comparison, musicians typically get a retweet for every thirty thousand followers. "We see a very high level of engagement with religious and spiritual content," a Twitter spokeswoman told CNN. "Followers respond to these topics with replies, retweets, and clicks on links much more often than they do other subjects."[2]

The *New York Times* originated this study, stating:

Why are some tweets more popular than others? When a Twitter staff member set out to answer that question 10 months ago, he thought the answer would emerge among posts from NBA players, politicians or actors. Instead, he found a mystery: a set of messages that were ricocheting around Twitter being forwarded and responded to at a rate that was off the charts.

"They were punching way above their weight," said Robin Sloan, who discovered the anomaly but did not recognize the names behind the tweets.

Joyce Meyer, Max Lucado, and Andy Stanley were not well known inside Twitter's offices. But they had all built loyal ranks of followers well beyond their social networks—they were evangelical Christian leaders whose inspirational messages of God's love perform about 30 times as well as Twitter messages from pop culture powerhouses like Lady Gaga.[3]

What Would George Whitefield, Jonathan Edwards, John Wesley, and Charles Finney Do?

If the "greats" were with us today, what would they say when they saw what we see? After years and years of reading their journals, studying their biographies, and reading as many of their sermons and devotionals as I could get my hands on, I truly believe they would be absolutely floored by the activity of God around the world in our day.

These were men who lived in times of significant, history-making awakenings that transformed societies, and yet I believe they would say that what is happening in our day is greater and more significant than anything the human race has seen before. It's too bad that so many of us know so little when it comes to churches and ministries making a big impact in our communities for Christ. If you asked the average Christian on the street, he or she would only know a small percent of these great happenings around the world. That's why I want us to be mindful and purposeful when it comes to doing something, whatever the Lord impresses upon you to do, as you participate in this great movement happening now. We can no longer say we don't know about it, and we need to take seriously the kingdom work that God has called us to be a part of.

A Life of Discovery

I've committed myself to a life of discovery and celebration of God's activity around me and all around the world. Like a journalist with an exciting story to write, I'm always on the beat, searching for the story of what God is up to and how he really, practically cares for the world, and for every individual on earth.

A few years ago, I was on a trip to Pittsburgh to speak at several churches. The night Michelle and I arrived, we caught the tail end of an evening service. We enjoyed the spirit of worship in the host church and loved the classy look of the facilities. We happened to be at a church that is planting lots and lots of churches across their region. The lead pastor had arrived at the church a few decades earlier as a young pastor still in his twenties, and he continues to lead the congregation with a youthful vigor for the sake of the surrounding communities to know the gospel through life-giving communities of believers. He understands that it is not all up to his church alone, and so he invests at a level unheard-of by most churches to see the gospel disseminate and transform lives forever.

I introduced myself to a gentleman in the hallway following the service and enjoyed his European accent. For some reason, the conversation went to a recent trip we had taken to Calcutta, India, where we worked with a legendary missionary named Huldah Buntain. Huldah had been close friends with Mother Teresa and had even taken care of Mother Teresa in her dying days. Huldah had also planted over a thousand churches across India (more on Huldah's story later in the book).

To my amazement, this Swedish church leader with whom I happened to be sharing these recent experiences humbly began to reveal how God had been using him and his wife, and they had planted over a thousand churches across Northern Africa, Asia, and the Middle East in some of the most unreached areas of the world. You can't make this stuff up. Everywhere I go, every encounter I have, God shows another aspect of his movement, activity, and care for the world. He is at work; we should be working, too.

As I take you with me on this journey through the rest of this book, I sincerely hope and pray you will commit yourself to a life of discovery of God's activity around you, and learn to take notice and celebrate it. This will cultivate a life of thanksgiving and gratefulness to God. And out of this soil will grow a greater passion for God and for people.

Go to www.thinke.org for Challenge #2.

To Think About

1. What story speaks the most to you and why does it grip your heart?

2. Have you considered being a part of an overseas mission trip or starting a mission or outreach in your own neighborhood or to your kids' friends in your own home?

3. Why is story a more motivating factor than just simply hearing a message?

4. How will you help to make these stories and others you have read or heard of known to those you are in relationship with?

Notes

[1] Christina Chaey, "Does God Retweet?" *Fast Company,* December 4, 2012, accessed October 24, 2014, http://www.fastcompany.com/3003649/does-god-retweet.

[2] Eric Marrapodi and Ben Wedeman, "Pope opens a personal Twitter account," *belief Blog, CNN,* December 2, 2012, accessed October 24, 2014, http://religion.blogs.cnn.com/2012/12/02/pope-to-open-a-personal-twitter-account/comment-page-1/.

[3] Amy O'Leary, "Christian Leaders Are Powerhouses on Twitter," *New York Times,* June 2, 2012, accessed October 24, 2014, www.nytimes.com/2012/06/02/technology/christian-leaders-are-powerhouses-on-twitter.html.

Chapter Three

CAN YOU REALLY MISS SOMETHING SO IMPORTANT?

*I'm doing something right before your eyes that you
won't believe, though it's staring you in the face.*
—Acts 13:41 *The Message*

Michelle and I recently visited the Minneapolis Institute of Arts to view several authentic Terracotta Army figures excavated and recovered by archeologists from China. The intricacies and attention to detail on these life-size figures is astounding. It was one of the most enjoyable museum trips we have taken.

The Terracotta Army is a relatively new find by historians, first unearthed in 1974 by local farmers who were digging a water well to the east of Xi'an in the Shaanxi province, after two millennia of being hidden underground. (Interestingly, *Xian* is actually an ancient, shortened term for the word Christian.) To everyone's surprise, these farmers had unearthed part of what we now know to be the largest archeological dig in the world. Archeologists estimate that the three pits contain life-size figures of nine thousand soldiers, chariots, and horses, the majority of which are still being uncovered. According to one historian,

Chinese workers began assembling the Terracotta Army shortly after the first Emperor of China ascended to his throne, and its construction eventually involved nearly three quarters of a million workers. This army was created to be buried with the emperor, to protect him in his afterlife.

This historic clay army had been right under their noses for thousands of years.

To put the number of workers in perspective, it took about seventy thousand men to dig the Panama Canal, of which more than twenty-seven thousand died in the process from malaria and yellow fever due to large mosquito populations. According to the Greek historian Herodotus, one hundred thousand men were engaged in building the pyramids in Egypt, though many historians estimate there were fewer workers than this.

The Terracotta Army had been unknown until it was unearthed, yet it is nearly ten times the size of either of these feats of mankind: the Panama Canal or the Egyptian Pyramids. Here the Terracotta Army had been, right under their noses all this time. It hadn't made the news because nobody had heard about it yet. But imagine their surprise when they found it!

As with the Terracotta Army, we have moves of God of biblical proportions happening all around us that we need to unearth and make known to the American church. Our problem is that so many of us view our Christian faith through the lens of our local church, our denomination, the churches across our region, or the sporadic news we hear about other churches or movements around the world. And we write in our subconscious journal: "Nothing important is happening," or "Very little is happening," while in reality amazing things are taking place right under our noses. We just haven't heard of them yet. We haven't looked outside our very small circles of understanding.

We have to learn to assume that much more is happening than we realize—many better, more exciting things, if we could only discover them.

The World Used to Be Flat

Can we really miss something so important? Let me take you down a rabbit trail for a few stories—stories outside the Christian realm, but important and recognizable nonetheless. As you'll notice, we humans miss big things all the time. And this is not limited to the spiritual realm. Just because something is really important doesn't necessarily mean it gets noticed.

And what better place to start than with the fact that humans used to think the world was flat?

Simon Sinek writes in his book *Start with Why* about assumptions and why they matter:

> Our behavior is affected by our assumptions or our perceived truths. We make decisions based on what we think we know. It wasn't too long ago that the majority of people believed the world was flat. This perceived truth impacted behavior. During this period, there was very little exploration. People feared that if they traveled too far, they might fall off the edge of the earth. So for the most part they stayed put. It wasn't until that minor detail was revealed— the world is round—that behaviors changed on a massive scale. Upon this discovery, societies began to traverse the planet. Trade routes were established; spices were traded. New ideas, like mathematics, were shared between societies, which unleashed all kinds

of innovations, and advancements. The correction
of a simple false assumption moved the human race
forward.[1]

Amazing, isn't it? Imagine what you and I have missed when
we fall into the same trap. Our assumptions cause us to miss
important truths all the time.

The First Flight Didn't Make the New York Times

Sinek shares later on in his book about the race to see who could
build the world's first heavier-than-air flying machine at the end
of the nineteenth century. Two camps were working towards the
first flight. The first was one of the best-known men in the field,
funded and staffed by the federal government: Samuel Pierpont
Langley. The *New York Times* was literally following him around
as he worked towards a flying machine. The second team we all
know today, but they looked far less likely to succeed in their day:

> A few hundred miles away in Dayton, Ohio, Orville
> and Wilbur Wright were also building a flying
> machine. Unlike Langley, the Wright brothers did
> not have the recipe for success. There was no funding
> for their venture. No high-level connections. The
> Wright brothers funded their dream with the pro-
> ceeds from their bicycle shop. Not a single person
> working on the team, including Orville and Wilbur,
> had a college education: some did not even finish high
> school. . . . Every time the Wright brothers went out
> to make a test flight, so the stories go, they would take
> five sets of parts with them, because they knew that's
> how many times they were likely to fail before decid-
> ing to come home for the day.

Then it happened. On December 17, 1903, on a field in Kitty Hawk, North Carolina, the Wright brothers took to the sky. A fifty-nine second flight at an altitude of 120 feet at the speed of a jog was all it took to usher in a new technology that would change the world.

Remarkable as it was, it went relatively unnoticed. The New York Times was not there to cover the story.[2]

This boggles my mind. Just think about that for a minute. The Wright Brothers did it. They finally attained the age-old human desire to be airborne, and the major newspapers weren't there to report on it. Unbelievable, really.

It wasn't until nearly fifty years later that the commercial airline industry was born. As it was, for decades following the Wright Brothers' breakthrough, the airplane was seen only as a war instrument and, beyond that, a silly toy. What we have seen in industrial innovation through the course of American history, we also see in spiritual realities today. Often, historic opportunities are passed up and squandered for a season simply due to our lack of knowledge that it's important news.

The Wright Brothers were legends, but for years no one truly realized the significance of what was taking place. This is what it means to live awake: to take notice of the significant things God is doing in churches and places all over the world. We don't need to wait for decades to recognize that God was moving and we missed the time of his visitation.

Bach Was Not "Bach" Back in His Lifetime

The composer Johann Sebastian Bach was not given the honor due him during his lifetime.

> During his lifetime, [the composer] Telemann
> enjoyed a fame that far surpassed that of his contem-
> porary, J. S. Bach. Not only was he considered to be
> the better musician—he was compensated accordingly
> with a salary in Hamburg at least three times larger
> than Bach's in Leipzig. . . .
>
> Bach's contemporaries had all but dismissed him
> as old-fashioned by the time of his death in 1750. . . .
> The true revival of Bach's works began in 1829, how-
> ever, when Mendelssohn conducted a famous perfor-
> mance of the St. Matthew Passion in Berlin. After
> hearing the performance, Hegel called Bach a "grand,
> truly Protestant, robust and, so to speak, erudite
> genius which we have only recently learned again to
> appreciate at its full value." Mendelssohn's efforts to
> promote Bach's music continued, and eventually led
> to the founding of the Bach . . . Society, an organiza-
> tion devoted exclusively to promoting his works.[3]

Where would we be without the music of Bach? Sadly, many other geniuses in the world of music and art are probably being skipped over as well; many remain yet to be uncovered, to our detriment.

What Bach did for the musical world, many men and women of God are doing in the spiritual world, and yet they are being passed over because we don't yet recognize the genius of what the Spirit of God is doing through their lives. As they have lived awakened to God and his purposes, they have given us a chance, a window, and an opportunity to peer into what it looks like for us to live awake to the great purposes and promises of God over our lives.

Banksy Street Art Hardly Sells

Another most-interesting documentary is about a street artist named Banksy. He has become so renowned in the UK that his original works of art sell for hundreds of thousands of dollars.

Banksy has built his reputation on practical jokes. The *New York Daily News* reports that in 2013, he set up a stall in Central Park in New York City with some of his original artwork, which would typically sell for hundreds of thousands of dollars, and priced them at sixty dollars each. He captured this all with a camera and posted the video online the next day. It was hours before his first sale. Banksy reported, "'A lady buys two small canvases for her children, but only after negotiating a 50% discount. . . .' A man from Chicago . . . who [said] that he just needed 'something for the walls' of his new house walked away with four paintings. . . . The stunt netted $420." [4]

Simply because they didn't realize it, and the artist didn't try to help them realize it, customers paid sixty dollars for art pieces worth hundreds of thousands of dollars each! Talk about winning the lottery.

The truth is you don't know what you don't know. The same is true of spiritual treasure. Most Christians aren't even close to realizing what they've been given in the gospel. Scripture actually tells us that this is the case. Paul writes:

> I pray Christ will be more and more at home in your hearts, living within you as you trust in him. May your roots go down deep into the soil of God's marvelous love; and may you be able to feel and understand, as all God's children should, how long, how wide, how deep, and how high his love really is; and to experience this love for yourselves, *though it is so*

great that you will never see the end of it or fully know or understand it. And so at last you will be filled up with God himself. (Eph. 3:17–19 TLB; italics mine)

And though we may not understand it, Paul is calling us to continue to search the deepness of God's love. And, as we've discovered, a significant part of grasping God's love is noticing how he is outworking his love in stories all around us. Not to be missed, there is a sense that to the depth that we have spiritual vision to see the love of God, to that depth we will be filled with the fullness of God.

There Is Deep Scriptural Precedent That God Is at Work

There is deep Scriptural precedent promising every believer that God is working all around us more than we grasp or can conceive. As Acts 13:41 says, "I'm doing something right before your eyes that you won't believe, though it's staring you in the face" (*The Message*). Read and ponder a few important Bible promises on God's immense activity.

- Jesus did many other things as well. If every one of them were written down, I suppose that even the whole world would not have room for the books that would be written. (John 21:25)
- Then said the Lord to me, You have seen well, for I am alert *and* active, watching over My word to perform it. (Jer. 1:12 AMP)
- Jesus said to them, "My Father is always at his work to this very day, and I too am working." (John 5:17)
- Of the greatness of his government and peace there will be no end. (Isa. 9:7)

- . . . I will build my church; and the gates of Hades will not overpower it. (Matt. 16:18b NASB)
- LORD my God, You have done many things—Your wonderful works and Your plans for us; none can compare with You. If I were to report and speak of them, they are more than can be told. (Ps. 40:5 HCSB)
- My mouth will tell of your righteous acts, of your deeds of salvation all day long, though their number is past my knowledge. (Ps. 71:15 NRSV)

The Thing about Spiritual Vision

As believers, there shouldn't be any more doubt in our minds that God is active. In fact, we need to learn to doubt our doubts and have faith in our faith. Scripture promises us over and over again that God is at work all around us. It encourages us that God's goodness and good works are greater than we comprehend or count.

Two statements deeply impacted me this year. Rich Langton, Creative Pastor at Hillsong church, wrote: "God doesn't just do good, He's the definition of good. Everything we think of as good, ultimately reflects Him."[5] All the good we see in the world is a gift from God. All the evil has come through the devil and humanity's sinfulness. We have to grasp that God's goodness is true and beautiful. David Sliker of the International House of Prayer wrote: "When this season of life is finished and our full story is told, we will not have even one small complaint with the leadership of God."[6] The thing about God is that he can turn even our pain into something good. We often don't see it at the time, but sometimes we look in hindsight on our experiences and catch a glimpse of God's perfect ways. He redeems us, and he redeems our circumstances. Everything about God is good.

But we humans like to deflate the goodness of God and inflate our own goodness. *Society tells us the closer we get to God, the more we realize the divinity within ourselves. The gospel tells us the closer we get to God, the more we realize the depravity within ourselves.* If we're not careful, we start to think God is the bad one and we are the good ones. This could not be further from the truth. Jesus said the man who is justified before God is the one who says: "God, have mercy on me, a sinner." When we recognize our imperfection, then and only then do we start to see who God really is and what God really does in our lives. Peter Haas sums up this truth by saying, "Grace cannot invade a self-sufficient heart."[7]

The thing about spiritual vision is that because of our sinfulness we lose sight of God, and because of our pain we begin to mistrust God. When we finally repent of our sin and forgive those who have hurt us—as God calls us to do over and over again in his Word—then the light of God shines like a bright, healing beam in our hearts and clears the vision of God before us.

On the Ground at Ground Zero

Let me give you a further example of this. When I first met my wife Michelle, we were really drawn to each other, and we spent as much time together as we could that first summer. I must've made a good impression, because she invited me on her family vacation to New York City toward the end of the summer.

I hadn't traveled much growing up with my family, except for a dozen annual trips to South Dakota. But not South Dakota like you might think. We traveled into South Dakota just across the border from Minnesota. We vacationed there so my uncle could be close to his farm and care for his cows. Still to this day, I haven't seen Mount Rushmore, the Black Hills, or Sturgis (the three main attractions in the state). We would always set up tents and camp at a lake resort near where my relatives lived. So you can imagine how cooped up I had been, and I definitely felt the itch to travel and see other parts of the world.

A few weeks before the 9/11 terrorist attacks, in August of 2001, we traveled to and toured New York City with Michelle's family: we went to Broadway shows, ate at great restaurants, and paid way too much for a tiny hotel room, but such is New York City. Michelle and I even managed to capture a picture with the World Trade Center in the background as we were ferrying to the Statue of Liberty. I don't know about you, but it is still eerie seeing the Twin Towers in old movies.

Weeks later, the tragedy of our times befell New York City . . . and our nation. Thousands lost their lives just blocks from where we had walked a few weeks earlier, and our nation wept together at the evil in the world. I truly don't think I grasped what occurred on 9/11. I still remember exactly where I was—I was in Bible college at the time—but the depth of what was taking place escaped my young mind.

It wasn't until years later, the first time we visited Ground Zero after 9/11, that I believe I truly grasped the magnitude of the loss and tragedy. We walked through the underground subway tunnels, passing by soldiers with guns draped over their shoulders. We slowly climbed the stairs up to where the gaping holes stood in the middle of this great city, and I was floored. Even after watching it on TV for years, and reading what felt like every article we could get our hands on, there was no substitute for seeing it in front of our eyes. Nothing could replace that feeling. It was more real than it had ever been before. My heart mourned again for so much loss.

We can see something, but not really see it. We catch a glimpse of it, but we don't really grasp it. The magnitude of what is taking place eludes us. People often have this eye-opening experience on short-term mission trips. They've heard of the poor, they've seen commercials on TV, or driven by a beggar on the street, but when they actually walk with the poor and do life with the poor, it transforms them in a way that is hard to describe. It would be difficult to overemphasize the difference between knowing about the poor and actually knowing the poor.

This blindness happens in our spiritual lives all the time. We read the Scripture, but the depth and meaning eludes us. We hear about God moving around the world, but we don't really understand what's happening. It is more than just an information-transfer issue; we all struggle with varying degrees of spiritual blindness to the ways and workings of God.

In his second letter to the church in Corinth, Paul teaches about the Light that comes from God, which helps us overcome our spiritual blindness so that we can see the Lord's goodness:

> The old way, with laws etched in stone, led to death, though it began with such glory that the people of Israel could not bear to look at Moses' face. For his face shone with the glory of God, even though the brightness was already fading away. Shouldn't we expect far greater glory under the new way, now that the Holy Spirit is giving life? If the old way, which brings condemnation, was glorious, how much more glorious is the new way, which makes us right with God! In fact, that first glory was not glorious at all

compared with the overwhelming glory of the new way. So if the old way, which has been replaced, was glorious, how much more glorious is the new, which remains forever!

Since this new way gives us such confidence, we can be very bold. We are not like Moses, who put a veil over his face so the people of Israel would not see the glory, even though it was destined to fade away. *But the people's minds were hardened, and to this day whenever the old covenant is being read, the same veil covers their minds so they cannot understand the truth. And this veil can be removed only by believing in Christ.* . . .

But whenever someone turns to the Lord, the veil is taken away. For the Lord is the Spirit, and wherever the Spirit of the Lord is, there is freedom. So all of us who have had that veil removed can see and reflect the glory of the Lord. And the Lord—who is the Spirit— makes us more and more like him as we are changed into his glorious image. . . .

If the Good News we preach is hidden behind a veil, it is hidden only from people who are perishing. Satan, who is *the god of this world, has blinded the minds of those who don't believe. They are unable to see the glorious light of the Good News. They don't understand this message about the glory of Christ*, who is the exact likeness of God. . . .

For *God*, who said, "Let there be light in the darkness," *has made this light shine in our hearts so we could know the glory of God that is seen in the face of Jesus Christ.* (2 Cor. 3:7–4:6 NLT; italics mine)

Many Missed Jesus When He Walked among Them

Think about this for a minute while considering the idea of spiritual blindness. Many people walked by Jesus unaware—the Son of God in the flesh. Sure, some enjoyed his miracles, but often crowds walked away at the first hint of hard teaching. It's no surprise, then, that many of us miss the astounding life change God is doing around us or have trouble understanding the real significance of the gospel.

Jesus is the One about whom Scripture says:

In these final days, he has spoken to us through his Son. God promised everything to the Son as an inheritance, and through the Son he created the universe. The Son radiates God's own glory and expresses the very character of God, and he sustains everything by the mighty power of his command. When he had cleansed us from our sins, he sat down in the place of honor at the right hand of the majestic God in heaven. This shows that the Son is far greater than the angels, just as the name God gave him is greater than their names. (Heb. 1:2–4 NLT)

And

The Son is the image of the invisible God, the firstborn over all creation. For in him all things were created: things in heaven and on earth, visible and invisible, whether thrones or powers or rulers or authorities; all things have been created through him and for him. He is before all things, and in him all things hold together. And he is the head of the body, the church; he is the beginning and the firstborn from among the dead, so that in everything he might have

the supremacy. For God was pleased to have all his
fullness dwell in him, and through him to reconcile to
himself all things, whether things on earth or things
in heaven, by making peace through his blood, shed
on the cross. (Col. 1:15–20)

And yet people walked by Jesus unaware, unfazed by his unas-
suming glory. There is not much that depicts our spiritual blindness more than this one simple fact: people missed Jesus walking
on the earth. Even Jesus was amazed at the lack of spiritual
vision when he exclaimed: "You did not recognize the time of
God's coming to you" (Luke 19:44). Hundreds of years earlier,
it was prophesied this would happen: "Because they regard not
the works of the Lord nor the operations of His hands, He will
break them down and not rebuild them" (Ps. 28:5 AMP).

Before we get too hasty to point fingers at those who do not
see spiritual truth, we must remember that *even those who loved
and followed Jesus often missed the significance of his miracles.* Mark
6:52 in the Amplified Bizble reads of one such instance after Jesus
fed thousands with only a small portion of food. In dramatic
fashion, God multiplied what little was there to feed the hungry
crowd. "For they failed to consider *or* understand [the teaching
and meaning of the miracle of] the loaves; [in fact] their hearts
had grown callous [had become dull and had lost the power of
understanding]."

Then, following Jesus's resurrection from the dead, he
appeared to several men walking on the road to Emmaus—they
walked and talked with their Lord and still did not recognize
him. Only just before he left them were their eyes opened to
recognize who he really was.

Mary, a close follower of Jesus, came to his tomb to honor
his body after his death on the cross, and she did not recognize

him risen from the dead. She thought he was just another gardener, until he spoke her name.

At times, even Jesus's closest disciples missed the significance of what he was doing, showing us that spiritual blindness happens to the best of us to varying degrees.

It's amazing to think about, but only a small margin of people saw the glory of Christ while he walked the earth. This tells us it could be just as easy to miss the activity of his Holy Spirit all around us today. We need eyes to see what God is doing and the redemptive revelation of what he wants for our lives.

In his earlier letter to the church in Corinth, Paul writes about this spiritual vision problem for the believer: "Now we see things imperfectly, like puzzling reflections in a mirror, but then we will see everything with perfect clarity. All that I know now is partial and incomplete, but then I will know everything completely, just as God now knows me completely" (1 Cor. 13:12 NLT). While we are on this earth, we will never see God's truth with perfect clarity; we will only be able to see through a mirror dimly. But this shouldn't stop us from asking God to purify our hearts, clarify our vision, and awaken us to his goodness and glory, that we might follow him more fully. *The more clearly we see the reality and significance of the gospel, the more readily and heartily we worship.* Herein lies the reason we will never stop worshipping in heaven. In heaven, our spiritual blindness will be fully removed. We will finally see the glory of God for all its gusto, and our hearts will cry out in unending worship.

Why It Is So Important We See Better

We can't let the fact that we have trouble seeing keep us from trying. When we see God's truth and actively search for signs of his presence and working around the world, it awakens us and expands our hearts. Knowing what God is doing with others expands us—it fills our hearts and minds with greater faith and vision, and it ultimately draws us to the greater action that God has for us. 1 Thessalonians 3:8 states: "In the middle of our trouble and hard times here, just knowing how you're doing keeps us going. Knowing that your faith is alive keeps us alive" (*The Message*). Maybe you've felt this before? Billy Graham has said, "Most of the Christian life is spent in the valley."[8] Life does not always go our way, or the way we think it should. We have all experienced what Jesus's followers promised: "We must go through many hardships to enter the kingdom of God" (Acts 14:22). As Leonard Ravenhill reveals, Romans 8 starts with the promise that there will be no condemnation from God, and ends with the promise that there can be no separation from God, but it never says there will be no tribulation in between.[9] When we go through these valleys we are promised we will face, there is nothing better than a fresh story of God "moving a mountain" for someone else to help us muster the faith to trust God until we see a change in our own circumstances. Hearing how others are doing keeps us going. Knowing other people whose faith is alive keeps us alive.

It is never by accident that we hear about what God is doing in some corner of the world—God wants to continue to lift us to a new place of productivity for his kingdom and to beckon us to those outside the church that he longs for us to reach with the gospel. Proverbs 29:18 expresses the importance of this: "Where there is no vision [no redemptive revelation of God], the people perish" (AMP). We need a growing vision of the redemptive revelation of God, so we can be ushered into his greater purposes for our lives.

Here's an important question: How can you believe God is for you, if you never see God at work around you in simple, practical ways? It is his day-to-day work all around us that sears the truth of his being "for us" into the depths of our souls. We need to hear these stories.

Let's awaken together to the power and glory of God's story. Let's not miss something so important. Scripture calls out to us today: "Awake, O sleeper, and arise from the dead, and Christ will shine on you" (Eph. 5:14b ESV). We have a part, and God has a part. May we live every day of our lives awakened to the undercurrent of God's story all around us, and may the next section's "Live Inspired" stories expand our hearts to greater faith, vision, encouragement, and action.

Go to www.thinke.org for Challenge #3.

To Think About

1. Do you believe important stories happen all the time without you ever hearing of them?

2. Have you ever thought about the difference between knowing about God and knowing God personally? Where are you in this spectrum?

3. What do you think keeps people from recognizing what God is doing in so many lives today?

4. What are some ways you can clear your spiritual vision, so that you can be more attuned to what God is doing with others and, ultimately, what he wants to do in and through your life?

Notes

[1] Simon Sinek, *Start with Why: How Great Leaders Inspire Everyone to Take Action* (New York: Portfolio Trade, 2011): 11–12.

[2] Ibid., 96–98.

[3] "Major Baroque Composers," Music of the Baroque, www.baroque.org/baroque/composers.htm.

[4] Bill Hutchinson, "Graffiti Artist Banksy Said He Sold Original Pieces for Cheap in Central Park," *New York Daily News,* October 14, 2013, www.nydailynews.com/new-york/banksy-sells-original-pieces-cheap-central-park-article-1.1484557.

[5] Rich Langton, May 16, 2013, accessed October 27, 2014, https://twitter.com/RichLangton/status/335230699734986752.

[6] David Sliker, May 17, 2013, accessed October 27, 2014, https://twitter.com/davidsliker/status/335403704008179712.

[7] Peter Haas, December 15, 2012, accessed October 27, 2014, https://www.facebook.com/evangelistmatt/posts/440370129364007.

[8] As told to me personally by a thirty-year staff member while working at the Billy Graham Evangelistic Association.

[9] Leonard Ravenill, copyright © 1995 by Leonard Ravenhill, Lindale, Texas, http://www.ravenhill.org/conqr.htm.

Section Two

LIVE INSPIRED

Chapter Four

HEAVEN TOUCHING EARTH (PRAYER MOVEMENTS)

You will seek me and find me
when you seek me with all your heart.

—Jeremiah 29:13

As Michelle and I were finishing our college studies in Minneapolis, I applied for a scholarship for ministry majors provided by a generous donor to our university, which offered several free trips to Israel for graduating students. I had always wanted to visit Israel, and I expressed this desire in the one-page form. I won the trip. Visiting Israel in person on this scholarship trip was quite possibly the most incredible travel experience Michelle and I have had. Between us, we've been to dozens of countries, but there was something unique, potent, and mystical about visiting Israel.

One of the many highlights of our trip was visiting the mountain where Jesus was transfigured in front of his three closest disciples: Peter, John, and James. Thankfully, we were able to drive up in a car, because it would have been a long hike. Perhaps no story shows such a brilliant example of heaven touching earth as this story about Jesus.

Luke shares this story—Peter, John, and James go with Jesus up a mountain where he is transfigured in front of their eyes:

> About eight days after Jesus said this, he took Peter, John and James with him and went up onto a mountain to pray. As he was praying, the appearance of his face changed, and his clothes became as bright as a flash of lightning. Two men, Moses and Elijah, appeared in glorious splendor, talking with Jesus. They spoke about his departure, which he was about to bring to fulfillment at Jerusalem. Peter and his companions were very sleepy, but *when they became fully awake, they saw his glory* and the two men standing with him. As the men were leaving Jesus, Peter said to him, "Master, it is good for us to be here. Let us put up three shelters—one for you, one for Moses and one for Elijah." (He did not know what he was saying.)
>
> While he was speaking, a cloud appeared and covered them, and they were afraid as they entered the cloud. A voice came from the cloud, saying, "This is my Son, whom I have chosen; listen to him." When the voice had spoken, they found that Jesus was alone. The disciples kept this to themselves and did not tell anyone at that time what they had seen. (Luke 9:28–36; italics mine)

When we went up to visit the Mount of Transfiguration on our trip to Israel, we found that they now have three churches at this spot. I think they may have missed the point of this passage.

Scripture says when these three close companions of Christ "became fully awake, they saw his glory." This is what we need more than anything today. When we become fully awake, we will see God for who he really is, and be amazed. We need God to open our eyes. We need to be willing for him to shatter our paradigms and open us up to the wonders of his gospel. When we become fully awake, inspiration will fill our hearts and drive us to take new ground for the cause of Christ. Just as a car can't drive without gas in the tank, if we don't live awake by opening ourselves up to see God's activity, inspiration can't flow in like gas to fuel us to the places God wants us to go.

We need not get discouraged when we sense we are not awake to the purposes of God. It is simply a reminder—like a fuel gauge on empty—to ask God to open our eyes. It is always encouraging to read about the twelve disciples who were Jesus's closest followers. Over and over again they are putting their foot in their mouths and being rebuked by Jesus. It gives us hope for our own failings today. The Bible shows us over and over again that we don't need to be perfect in order for God to use us.

My Purpose in Sharing These Stories

My purpose in sharing all the stories in this book is solely to point to God. I really don't want to create hero-worship; I simply want to create God-worship. My hope for you is not that you will copy one of the "Live Inspired" stories in the following chapters, but rather that you will let them stir something deeper in you—a trust in God's hand in your life in a unique way. That he is the one writing your story for his glory.

On the Mount of Transfiguration, God spoke clearly that *it is not about men's or women's stories; it is about his Son Jesus's story.* "In the past God spoke to our ancestors through the prophets at many times and in various ways, but in these last days he has spoken to us by his Son, whom he appointed heir of all things, and through whom also he made the universe" (Heb. 1:1–2). So let's not try to build shelters on the spot as we read these stories. Instead, let's let them inspire us toward Jesus's goodness and truth and to know him more.

I purposefully don't want to point you to individuals and lift up their ministries or leadership. At times, these specifics will be essential to the story. Mostly, I just want you to see there are more stories than you or I could ever count. Picture Alex Thomson in the midst of the ocean waves on his solo yacht race around the world. Like the waves crashing over on every side, making him realize how insignificant he really is, God is at work around us on every side, showing that this story is always bigger than we are. The stories point us to how big God really is, and how able he is to keep his Word. It's not about a single wave—even a really high or powerful wave. The waves, the "Live Inspired" stories, are meant to point to God's bigger story in his Son, Jesus, because ultimately that's the only story worth sharing.

John, who walked with Jesus, tells us, "Jesus did many other things as well. If every one of them were written down, I suppose that even the whole world would not have room for the books that would be written" (John 21:25). If Jesus did more in three years of earthly ministry than can be written on all the pages of all the books of the world, what do you think Jesus has done over the thousands of years since, and how much do you think he is doing today? *There are still not enough books in the world to completely capture all he is doing.*

Abraham was the father of all who have faith in the true God. His story was ultimately all about pointing at God's story. Listen in as *The Message* explains:

If Abraham, by what he did for God, got God to approve him, he could certainly have taken credit for it. *But the story we're given is a God-story, not an Abraham-story.* What we read in Scripture is, "Abraham entered into what God was doing for him, and that was the turning point. He trusted God to set him right instead of trying to be right on his own." If you're a hard worker and do a good job, you deserve your pay; we don't call your wages a gift. But if you see that the job is too big for you, that it's something only God can do, and you trust him to do it—you could never do it for yourself no matter how hard and long you worked—well, that trusting-him-to-do-it is what gets you set right with God, by God. Sheer gift. (Rom. 4:1–5; italics mine)

When We Pray, God Moves

It's no coincidence that Jesus was transfigured as he prayed. Possibly nothing helps us to see it is all about God's bigger story better than prayer. Leonard Ravenhill once said, "Some preachers strut in the pulpit, but never did a person strut in the prayer closet." Prayer confesses our absolute dependence on God and his mighty hand in our lives. If he doesn't show up, all our efforts are fruitless and futile. We continually need God to do what only he can do. So we pray, and then we pray some more.

Personal prayer is such an important part of the life of a Christian. Equally as important is corporate prayer. There is a sense of God's blessing that we don't experience in personal prayer, which we can only experience through praying together with other Christians. A. T. Pierson said, "There has never been a spiritual awakening in any country or locality that did not begin in united prayer." John Wesley said, "God does nothing except in response to believing prayer."

In the following chapters, I hope to help you live inspired through the stories of awakened people who are actively pursuing the purposes of God for our generation. The three visible movements of awakening that will be explored in the next few chapters are prayer, justice, and proclaiming the gospel.

His Life Was Defined by Prayer

Out of all the stories in the Bible, one of the most inspiring on persistent prayer is the story of Daniel. When you read his story, you see that Daniel's whole life was defined by prayer. After reading the book of Daniel again recently, I shared on my blog the first thing I took away: "Daniel knew how to get serious with God, and God took him seriously." Daniel didn't just pray a little bit; he prayed "through" until God clearly responded.

There are various instances of God's response to Daniel's praying. In Daniel 9, he prays and God answers immediately. But in Daniel 10, he prays daily for three weeks for one specific need. Finally, an angel of the Lord shows up and tells him that the answer was given immediately, but angels were warring in the heavenlies until that moment of breakthrough. One of my online friends wrote on my wall in response to my post: "When angels come and tell you they're sorry it took so long, you know you're doing something right." Author Mark Batterson has said: "We need to stop praying ASAP prayers and start praying ALAIT prayers" (as long as it takes). This is the kind of praying that captures the heart of God, and instills awakening within our souls. Sometimes we need to keep on praying until God moves.

The Breakthrough Comes through Prayer

Powerful praying is often linked to justice and preaching the gospel. We work to help the poor, free captives, and tell our cities about the love of God, but we also pray for all these efforts like it depends on God.

Moving Mountains, a little book put together by the Assemblies of God about intercessory prayer for missionaries, shares story after story of the power of praying when God burdens our hearts for missionaries. One story shares,

> The message written on the Christmas greeting surprised me. "What happened to you last February?" the writer asked. "One day as I was returning from work the Lord impressed me to pray for you. I felt that you were in mortal danger." I turned the card over. Its sender was a man in Arizona. As far as I could remember I had never met the man or heard from him before. But I certainly remembered what had happened to me the preceding February! I had gone with Theagene, one of our district presbyters, to minister in a remote region of southwest Haiti. We had started very early and traveled on horseback for hours to reach a mountain village in time for an afternoon service. When we arrived the mud-and-thatch church was full of people, many of whom had walked for hours to attend this meeting. That afternoon we enjoyed a blessed time of worship.
>
> After we dismissed the service, Theagene and I were approached by a pastor whose church was a two-hour journey further into the mountains. Knowing how seldom we were able to reach this area, he begged

us to go on to his church for another service while
we were so near. In fact, he had already announced
to his congregation that we would come! Although it
was late and we were hours away from the little town
of Belle Riviere where we were to spend the night,
we could not disappoint him by refusing his request.
When we reached his church we found that it too
was filled with people. They had walked over some of
Haiti's roughest terrain to be in the service. Theagene
and I ministered to them, and God sent another gracious outpouring of His Spirit. When this service
concluded it was very late in the afternoon. Theagene
and I started back to Belle Riviere. Soon we were
riding through pitch-black darkness. Cautiously we
picked our way along a trail that followed the brink of
a ravine. We knew there were drop-offs of up to five
hundred feet. It had been a long day, and my horse
had stood for hours in the heat without water or food.
Suddenly he went berserk and started to run. I tried
to rein him in but it was impossible. I could only cling
to the saddle and in desperation cry out, "Jesus! Jesus!"
The horse ran full speed through the darkness down
that precipitous trail. I knew that the slightest misstep
would plunge us both to our deaths. For two hours,
I was hurtled through that starless night. Theagene,
hurrying to keep up, was unable to do anything to help.

When we finally reached Belle Riviere and the
horses stopped, we were exhausted and trembling.
But we were safe. This, I knew was a miracle. But I
had not realized the extent of the miracle until I read
the message on that Christmas greeting. Impressed

by the Holy Spirit that I was in danger, this man had gone home, fallen on his knees, and prayed. For two hours he interceded for me until he was assured by the Spirit that the danger, whatever it had been, was past. He mentioned the time, and it was the very same two hours when my horse had been racing so madly through the night. I rejoiced in the knowledge that God cared enough to alert someone to pray and that "someone" had been obedient to the promptings of the Spirit. Undoubtedly, this man's prayers had saved my life.[1]

God has done it before, and he wants to do it again through you and me. He is calling an army of people who will confess their dependency on him and be used by him to pray for awakening and his kingdom purposes on earth today. Do you want to be a part of this? Then let's dedicate ourselves again to prayer.

International House of Prayer

One of the most significant prayer movements in history is taking place in the heart of our nation, at a place known as the International House of Prayer. I personally have not attended, but I have met many of the leaders involved and have appreciated their godly, Christ-centered attitudes. Many good friends, as well as my mother, have traveled there for a few days or weeks at a time to spend extended time in prayer, and they have been deeply affected by the atmosphere of heaven that surrounds that place. It is such a vivid, modern-day portrayal of John Wesley traveling to the Moravians in Herrnhut, Germany, led by Count Zinzendorf, where his "heart was strangely warmed." The Moravians led a movement of prayer in Europe, including around-the-clock prayer, which lasted for more than one hundred years. Prayer movements like this tend to have an effect on ministers across the board. The increased presence of God does much good for both ministers and society.

The International House of Prayer (IHOP) writes about the story of their early days on their website: "In May of 1999, the International House of Prayer of Kansas City was founded by Mike Bickle and twenty full-time 'intercessory missionaries,' who cried out to God in prayer with worship for thirteen hours each day." Within months, the schedule had grown to include round-the-clock prayer for various team members, and this 24/7 prayer has continued since that time—now for fifteen years! They share about two biblical figures who inspire them in their mission,

> Anna, one of the first evangelists and intercessors in the New Testament, who prayed and fasted for over sixty years before Jesus' first coming (Luke 2:37), and King David who organized and paid four thousand musicians and nearly three hundred singers to worship God night and day. (1 Chron. 23:1–25:31)[2]

It is astonishing how this prayer movement has grown. There is an obvious hunger for God that is rising in the next generation. The International House of Prayer of Kansas City now hosts about two thousand believers who serve full time, investing fifty hours a week in prayer, outreach, service projects, and work in the classroom. These "intercessory missionaries" raise their own support to make this all possible.

Can you imagine a megachurch with thousands of people who do not just attend for one hour on a Sunday, but are each committing fifty hours a week in prayer, serving in the community, growing in their knowledge of Scripture, and proclaiming the gospel? Wow. Just wow.

Interestingly, in September of 2009, they began to combine round-the-clock prayer with round-the-clock acts of justice. "Outreach has always been a vital part of our mission. However, at that time . . . we are developing many new outreach ministries that will continue 24/7 alongside our 24/7 prayer and worship."

My mom has been to IHOP a dozen times. She describes the atmosphere of the around-the-clock prayer room and the conferences and worship services there as electric and charged with the tangible presence of God. She says that often when you go into the prayer room, you do not want to leave. I heard Matthew Barnett say, "The Presence of God is the answer to everything that keeps us up at night." It causes me to wonder: If our churches were charged with prayer until they were charged with the presence of God, would atheists walk in and immediately have their questions answered by the simple encounter with God's presence?

The International House of Prayer in Kansas City has been formational in developing and inspiring "houses of prayer" and other prayer movements across the United States and around the world, perhaps like at no other time in history. I am also told by several friends that multiple prayer movements other than the International House of Prayer opened around the same time and are also making a major impact. God has sovereignly brought them about in this important time in history. Many of the leaders I have met who are connected with various houses of prayer in our region and in other parts of the country are young, passionate, and living wholeheartedly for the Lord. They are dedicated to holiness, to prayer, to justice, and to the Word of God. They are building their lives around the gospel, and they are making a real difference in the world around them.

Passion Conferences

Contemporary worship music has been on a popular rise for the past few decades, and it has deeply influenced the current generation of Christians in America. Now Christian worship artists are creating anthems for the church-at-large and traveling across the country, drawing crowds larger than at any time in history to pray, worship, and seek the Lord together. It is fascinating to live in this time.

One large, well-known movement is the Passion Conferences, which started in 1997, calling college students to fast, pray, and worship along with other believers. This movement has grown and drawn hundreds of thousands of young people across the nation. These hundreds of thousands have been called to a life of purity, prayer, and dedication to Christ and the gospel.

It is through Passion Conferences that many people have come to know such worship artists as Chris Tomlin, Christy Nockels, Charlie Hall, Matt Redman, and David Crowder. Their albums and songs continue to build in prominence and impact more and more people. Their popularity creates a market that, in turn, opens opportunity for more and more rising worship artists to create their own anthems for the church as well.

New Year's Eve 2012

Over the past few years, multiple conferences drawing tens of thousands of young people have been put on simultaneously by Passion Movement, International House of Prayer, and Urbana Student Missions Conference. This is significant in so many ways, but especially powerful when we consider that they are drawing so many young people across our nation at the same time.

Around New Year's Eve in 2012, Urbana Student Missions Conference, which has taken place every three years since 1947, gathered sixteen thousand young people, many through the college ministry InterVarsity. The focus of the conference is asking young people to consider if God is calling them to give their lives to missions. It advocates an intense brand of Christian faith, calling young people to give their whole lives for the spread of God's gospel. Thousands respond to Christ (my friend York Moore has shared the gospel at each Urbana Conference over the past decade), and thousands are launched into a life of missionary service. The ripple effects are astounding and undeniable.

During that very same week, Passion Conferences took place in Atlanta, Georgia, and more than twenty-two thousand young people went to the Georgia Dome, where they spent full days in worship, prayer, and the preaching of God's Word. Well-known Christian artists led in worship, and the overriding theme was dedication to Christ and the gospel. Louie Giglio, the movement's founder, has stated: "Our heartbeat is to see the campuses of this nation awaken to God."[3]

Additionally, during that very same week, the International House of Prayer hosts their OneThing Conference (which my mom has attended the past few years), and in 2012, over twenty-five thousand young people gathered to fast and pray and seek God for our nation. Wonderfully, OneThing committed to praying and interceding for what God was doing at Urbana Missions Conference that year as well, showing the heartbeat between all these ministries is one—for the glory of Jesus Christ and his church.

Overall, at New Year's Eve of 2012, more than sixty thousand young people gathered on the same week in three cities across the nation. They worshiped, prayed, fasted, read the Scripture, and focused their lives on the gospel, justice, and missions. This is a vivid picture of the kind of prayer and worship that is taking place in the next generation today, and it should encourage every believer in our churches that God is not done yet.

The Practice of the Presence of God

We should let all these movements of prayer inspire us. Seeing the depths of other people's hunger for God should increase our own hunger for God. But what does prayer look like for the rest of us? Will we all be able to pray for hours? Is that even realistic? A good model for every Christian is seen in Brother Lawrence, whose devotional writing has influenced and encouraged believers for centuries. In his classic book, *The Practice of the Presence of God*, he shares how he began experiencing the same level of God's presence as he did simple chores like washing dishes for the brotherhood in his monastery as when he had dedicated prayer and solitude. God is available to all of us all the time in Christ. We have a backstage pass to God because of Jesus. We don't have to wait for devoted time to seek him. We can seek him right now, while we read this book, or tomorrow while we take our kids to soccer practice. Wherever we are, we only need to think of him and to worship him in our hearts—and we can experience his nearness.

Obviously, it would be wonderful if we could all set aside an hour each morning to study the Scripture and express our hearts to God, but for all the days we fail to keep this meeting with God, we only need to be still in whatever activity we find ourselves in throughout the day. We can be like Brother Lawrence and experience God in our workplace or while caring for our family. God is only waiting for our heart and thoughts to turn his direction, and he will come meet with us.

Go to www.thinke.org for Challenge #4.

To Think About

1. Have you seen God work in some significant way because you or someone you know prayed?

2. Are you regularly a part of any prayer meetings? What effect have they had on your relationship with God?

3. Is there an area of your life, or a need in your life, that you have given up praying for? How can you resolve to pray as long as it takes?

4. How can you dedicate yourself to God in prayer through-out the mundane moments of your day?

Notes

1 Joyce Wells Booze, *Moving Mountains: Intercessory Prayer in Missionary Ministry* (Springfield, MO: Assemblies of God, 1980), 61–63.

2 About page for the International House of Prayer, www.ihopkc.org/about.

3 Wanda Martin, "Passion 2012 – A Recap," *The Wartburg Watch*, January 6, 2012, thewartburgwatch.com/2012/01/06/passion-2012-a-recap.

Chapter Five

ON EARTH AS IT IS IN HEAVEN (JUSTICE MOVEMENTS)

Is not this the kind of fasting I have
chosen: to loose the chains of injustice
and untie the cords of the yoke, to set the
oppressed free and break every yoke?

—Isaiah 58:6

My friend Scott Noble has written for years for one of the premiere Christian newspapers in the country, and, before that, for *Decision Magazine*. In an article following the 2012 elections, he writes profoundly about the place of awakening within changing culture.

> Shortly after the election last month, Albert Mohler, president of the Southern Baptist Theological Seminary in Louisville, Kentucky, told the *New York Times*: "It's that the entire moral landscape has changed. . . ." Other evangelical leaders uttered similar opinions. All seemed to mark the most recent election results as a turning point in history—or at least a turning point for Christianity in America. I think they're missing the point, however. While elections

can help us ascertain the success or failure of certain political issues or candidates, they cannot predict the presence or direction of the Holy Spirit. . . .

And it's important to remember that Christianity—as a spiritual movement and as an individual life-changing force—mainly functions outside the halls of Washington, D.C. *The early church—arguably the most powerful and successful time in the history of the faith—operated outside the halls of power.* The faith and its followers were ridiculed, belittled, tortured and even martyred in a society with little respect for their beliefs. However, the number of believers grew, and the faith spread far outside of its early boundaries.

One could make the argument that during the previous 2,000 years, the times when the faith was most vibrant, the most life-changing, the most eternally-focused happened when it sat outside the embrace of the cultures it called home. While being politically aware and involved are certainly important, they are not what defines Christianity. The faith is defined by a life-changing relationship with Jesus Christ, which then leads to telling others about Him, helping the sick and downtrodden, fighting for justice and generally giving voice to those without one.[1]

The church has always been one of the greatest forces for good on the planet, and it continues to hold that kind of potential within its ranks. As we, empowered by God's Spirit, move from our church pews and respond to the proclamation of Scripture, we can save lives. Some would say it's great when governments get behind us and society as a whole picks up on the values of the Bible, but *God has always used his church whether or not the culture follows.*

Revival and awakening often occur outside the halls of power or without the popular newspapers of our day taking notice, and that's just fine. What God can do through one person completely sold out to him is more important than that. We don't need to wait for the right president, or the right congressmen, or the right media environment to pick up the cause of justice before we decide to do what is right in our own neighborhood, down the street, and on the other side of the world. *The person who follows Christ sees a need and fills it.* God has done too much inside of us for us to stay silent or spend all our time protesting—we want to actually do something to make a difference "with all the energy Christ so powerfully works" in us (Col. 1:29). God didn't do all that he has done inside of us so we could sit and coast through this life. He wants to use us to bring this life through to others.

What Does God Desire from Us?

The prophet Isaiah shares in no uncertain terms what God does and does not want from those who claim to follow him:

> "They act like a righteous nation that would never abandon the laws of its God. They ask me to take action on their behalf, pretending they want to be near me. 'We have fasted before you!' they say. 'Why aren't you impressed? We have been very hard on ourselves, and you don't even notice it!'
>
> "I will tell you why!" I respond. "It's because you are fasting to please yourselves. Even while you fast, you keep oppressing your workers. What good is fasting when you keep on fighting and quarreling?

101

This kind of fasting will never get you anywhere with me. You humble yourselves by going through the motions . . . .

"No, this is the kind of fasting I want: Free those who are wrongly imprisoned; lighten the burden of those who work for you. Let the oppressed go free, and remove the chains that bind people. Share your food with the hungry, and give shelter to the homeless. Give clothes to those who need them, and do not hide from relatives who need your help.

"Then your salvation will come like the dawn, and your wounds will quickly heal. Your godliness will lead you forward." (Isa. 58:2b–8 NLT)

Isaiah reminds us that God isn't interested in our spirituality or our church attendance if it is not backed up by treating others right. It's amazing because some people act as if America needs to get back to the olden days when religion was more prevalent, but we ignore the fact that the first settlers moved here and obliterated tribes of Native Americans, stealing their land. We too easily forget our horrific treatment of African slaves for nearly a century. The bitter traces of racism can still be seen throughout our nation.

I found out recently that my grandfather's grandpa lived in the time of Abraham Lincoln and the Civil War, when hundreds of thousands of Americans were killed by the hands of fellow citizens. That blows my mind. We have come so far in such a short time from my grandfather's grandfather, when millions of Americans took up arms against one another. American history, like that of all the other nations of the world, is blighted with these iniquities of disturbing treatment of other human beings created in the image of God. God desires us to spend our lives breaking all chains of injustice, serving and loving our fellow man as he has loved us, feeding the hungry, freeing people who are being trafficked, visiting the prisoner, clothing the poor, and speaking out for the oppressed. And while we may feel that we can't make much of a difference, we should do for one what we wish we could do for everyone. This is the kind of spirituality God wants from us.

Micah 6:8 encapsulates this kind of vibrant faith: "He has told you, O man, what is good; and what does the LORD require of you but to do justice, and to love kindness, and to walk humbly with your God?" (ESV).

More Justice Is Happening Than We Realize

Over and over again, I notice there's more justice happening than we realize. We met with a group of great friends during our second trip to the Catalyst Conference in Atlanta. We were spending time together sharing and learning about how to be more effective with online ministry. Thankfully, through a great connection, we were able to do our meet up at the Catalyst headquarters the day before the conference started. Some of the lab speakers at Catalyst made their way over to chat with us, and we brought in a few others who had great things to share. One of the leaders shared with us about his passion to innovate in the nonprofit sphere for good in his city. He was anxiously working to see justice with the poor in his city, and he shared how little he felt other organizations were doing.

I felt sorry for how little was happening in his city until a friend invited me out to coffee a few weeks later. He was with a friend of his from Thrivent Financial, which I came to learn is one of the largest faith-based philanthropic organizations in the world. They donate millions each year around the United States to meet needs, help the poor, and do good. He shared with me how many thousands of dollars are being invested even into cities like the one where we were told nothing was happening. The gentleman wanting to innovate and do justice in his city negated everything that was happening through organizations like Thrivent, simply because it was outside his denominational spectrum and because he had not heard of it yet.

Twenty-Seven Million in Slavery Today

One of the great needs rising to the top in churches today is modern-day slavery. It is hard to believe, but there are twenty-seven million men, women, and children trapped in slavery around the world, in brothels, factories, mines, and on street corners—human trafficking is even taking place under our noses in American cities.[2]

One amazing new movement has birthed out of Passion Conferences, and the young adults who gather each year to worship, called End It Movement. End It has worked to raise awareness of this great injustice, and it has built a coalition of major organizations such as International Justice Mission, the A21 Campaign, Not For Sale, and others who use rescue operations, legal action, governmental reform, police informing and support, and other methods to free people caught in trafficking. The church is at the forefront of this mission.

One of the challenges of this movement, along with other justice movements, is to describe how the average believer can be involved beyond simply raising awareness. I am so encouraged by how I see End It, International Justice Mission, and other organizations affecting culture and bringing freedom to the oppressed. This is a battle we all need to be part of with them. A good question to ask ourselves is: What if, instead of marching on Washington to contest more taxes, we marched and raised our voices to free modern-day slaves or to save the suffering in other parts of the world? Think of the change in mindset this would cause for those outside the church.

God's Heart Is Full of Compassion

I have been very blessed by Compassion International and their work with the poorest countries in the world. Michelle and I had the opportunity to spend a week in Santa Domingo, Dominican Republic, with them recently. We had heard of their great work, and we have partnered with them for our events. Over the years, we have been on many mission trips to some of the poorest areas of the world, but before we left, we prayed God would use this trip to do a continuing work in our hearts of love for the poor.

The Dominican Republic is an island nation in the Caribbean that is connected to Haiti. During our trip, we traveled to various projects and towns to see the work Compassion is doing in these poverty-stricken areas. The trip had a wonderfully personal feel, where we felt we actually got to know individuals in need on a personal level. We played with children at schools and visited a handful of families in their homes. The children and families we met were delightful. Their attitudes and thankfulness for the tiniest of gifts were astounding. The children who receive sponsorship through Compassion at around thirty-eight dollars per month were especially grateful for the written letters from their sponsors. They have so few people speaking hope into their lives. These letters from their sponsors provide a lifeline of hope and encouragement. I really would've never expected this. We have so much more than we realize in America, and that is not limited to financial resources.

In one home we sat in, in which twelve family members lived, the Compassion staff let us know "this young girl doesn't have a sponsor yet." Michelle and I said right then and there that we would like to sponsor her. Her name is Diana. We had an opportunity that less than one percent of Compassion sponsors ever get: to meet our child—and the even rarer opportunity to meet her right from the start of our choosing to sponsor her. She totally won our hearts. No longer was my desire to give to the poor vague: she now had a name. We had the sensation that we would've given her anything she asked for—providing for her was a complete joy.

We were absolutely amazed at the scope of Compassion's work. We saw that sponsoring a child is often more than a feeding program to provide extra nutrition and meals for these needy families. Sponsoring a child through Compassion quite literally breaks the cycle of poverty in a family that has lasted for generations. Over and over again, we met and talked with young adults who had been sponsored through Compassion and had grown up in the impoverished living conditions we saw Diana in, but who are now studying to be doctors, chiropractors, business leaders, and church leaders. It was mind-boggling for me to think that these young adults who were so well-spoken and had such bright futures, and who were already serving and becoming agents of change in their nation, had grown up in the conditions of poverty that we had witnessed with Diana. We met many formerly sponsored children who are now sponsoring children themselves, and through their vocational studies, they are beginning to help many others in their nation break out of cycles of poverty as well.

Compassion International is a Christ-centered organization. They have purposefully chosen to keep their tagline— "Releasing children from poverty in Jesus's name"—as part of their mission statement, even when watering it down could result in more public funding. Many don't realize that they are dedicated to an intrinsic partnership with the local church. All the children's daily education, discipleship, feeding programs, medical care, and sponsor gifts are facilitated by a local church in each community. From the get-go, these sponsored children are being educated in essential life skills, such as nutrition and how to get a good job when they get older. They are also being discipled for Christ from as early an age as four years old. Often, they end up coming to Christ, along with the rest of their family. The local church is able to provide ongoing care in a city for generations to come, and the community grows increasingly grateful to that local church for the care provided to these children and their families. This is an indescribably priceless partnership. Every child sponsored is building up the local church.

The breadth of Compassion to utterly transform a nation amazed me. In the Dominican Republic alone, Compassion has forty-five thousand sponsored children being fed, medically cared for, educated, and discipled. In Haiti, there are seventy thousand sponsored children. In India, there are 150,000 sponsored children. In total, twenty-six nations that meet specific criteria are focused on for child sponsorships by Compassion. Michelle and I found ourselves amazed at what God is doing with individual, formerly sponsored children who are now graduated from the program and becoming incredibly influential leaders in their nation. If God is doing that in one sponsored child, I can only begin to imagine what can God do with forty-five thousand of these children in a single nation. Compassion is one of the greatest evangelism and discipleship models I have ever seen. It is literally transforming nations one child at a time.

I believe there are several ways to bring justice that every American Christian should be involved with: supporting relief organizations when a natural disaster strikes somewhere in the world, filling up a shoebox through Operation Christmas Child during the Christmas season, and sponsoring a child through Compassion International. There are some things you don't need to pray about—"Lord, should I commit thirty-eight dollars a month to save a child's life through Compassion, break the cycle of poverty in their family, and influence a child who will eventually become a leader for change in their nation?" God's response was already given in Isaiah 58: stop praying about it and go change a life.

Find a Need and Fill It

Because of our focus on evangelism, I haven't been extensively involved with justice projects; but periodically, God has led my wife and me to meet a specific need. One winter, we were watching a CBS evening news story that shared about the great need in refugee camps bordering the war-torn nation of Syria. Thousands of refugees were flooding the camps, and the needs were massive. A businessman from Texas had begun overseeing one of the camps, and he expressed the need for shoes for the children during the harsh winter there.

Over two million Syrian refugees have fled from the crisis in their country into Jordan, Lebanon, and Turkey. Some of the refugees live in overcrowded, unsanitary, often dangerous camps, like Zaatari in northern Jordan—a camp established for thirty thousand people and now housing more than one hundred and fifty thousand men, women, and children. As conditions in the massive camps become more desperate, increasing numbers of refugees seek help outside the camps in urban areas, only to discover they have virtually no access to jobs, housing, education—or even food.

Fortunately, local churches and grassroots Christian organizations are providing some help to these refugees. These local heroes are offering desperate families groceries, clothing, shoes, first aid supplies, towels, blankets, mattresses, water filters, and heaters, particularly necessary now as winter temperatures reach record lows in the Middle East. In addition, these faithful servants deliver food and emergency supplies to displaced and vulnerable people still inside Syria, and they help to rescue Syrian women and girls from sex trafficking. All this work is done in the name and spirit of Jesus. The local people providing these services are unsung heroes.

I felt a great burden to come alongside these local heroes and do something to meet the great need of these Syrian refugees, but what can one person really do? Just hearing of the need broke my heart. I know there are a million problems in the world, but I had a strong sense that God wanted me to do something about this one in particular.

Knowing Lynne Hybels, the wife of Bill Hybels (pastor of Willow Creek Community Church in Chicago and convener of the Global Leadership Summit), was very involved in justice projects, I wrote her a note and asked if she would be willing to partner together and help us find the best use of funds if we were to do an online fundraising campaign for these needs. In her own words from her blog:

> A year ago I started reading news reports about the humanitarian crisis faced by millions—literally—of Syrian refugees chased by ongoing civil war across the borders of their country into Turkey, Lebanon and

Jordan. Analysts described it as the biggest human-
itarian crisis in decades, and first person reports
put faces to the men, women and children suffering
displacement, violence, and trauma. I knew I had to
do something. Matt sent me a note shortly before
Christmas. "I've got to do the fundraiser," Matt wrote.
"I'd appreciate your help, but with or without it, I have
to do this." Matt put together a crowd-funding page
and used his social networking expertise and con-
nections to get the word out about Syrian refugees. I
used my personal relationships in the Middle East to
identify grassroots Christian ministries in Jordan and
Lebanon that are serving Syrian refugees.[3]

As Lynne and I embarked on raising awareness and funds for
Syrian refugees, it ended far better than I had expected. I had
set out to raise ten thousand dollars, but together we raised
twenty-one thousand dollars in three weeks. One hundred
percent of the funds were directly given to meet the needs of
the refugees. Through our efforts, *The Christian Post*, Catalyst
Conference, Andy Stanley, and others shared about the project.
In the beginning, I wasn't sure I could do much, but I knew I had
to do something, and something was better than nothing. But
God took our humble efforts and made them more effective than
I could have dreamed. I know this amount is small compared to
the great needs of the refugees, but I pray it creates a ripple effect
in the Christian community across the nation that continues in
a groundswell of people playing whatever small part they can.

My heart continues to be burdened to do more financially
and also to pray for Syria. I love what Lynne posted since the
campaign: "For Syria: I pray that this war machine will crumble.

I don't know how or through whom this might happen. But I fast and I pray that it will."[4] Will you join with us in this prayer? Let's not stop until we see God do what only he can do. This is the kind of fasting God responds to—fasting and praying and giving and working and doing what we can do to see the oppressed set free.

How Much God Can Use One Person

I'm reminded of my time in Calcutta in early 2009. It wasn't the first time we had been to India; in fact, it was my third trip. Flying from Minneapolis, India is quite literally at the other end of the earth. No matter which direction you fly, east or west, it takes about twenty-four hours to arrive there.

On this trip, we spent over a week with Huldah Buntain, a close friend of the late Mother Teresa. Mother Teresa is well known to many. She was a Catholic nun who spent her life as a missionary in India. She specifically took care of the poorest of the poor, giving them dignity, care, and kindness in their dying days.

Not as many people know about Huldah Buntain, but Huldah was the one who took care of Mother Teresa in her own dying days. Huldah and her late husband Mark also spent their lives serving as missionaries in India. Together, they have planted a thousand churches throughout India, established over one hundred schools, and built one of the largest mission hospitals in the world in downtown Calcutta, known as Calcutta Mercy Hospital, where over forty thousand people each year are treated for free. They have also established a daily feeding program, which feeds tens of thousands of people every single day in various locations. Some of the children that have been saved off the streets through Huldah's work are now vice presidents at Starbucks and Mattel and doing other great things around the world. These were children who had been saved from a life of poverty and pain and were thrust into all the opportunity in the world—thanks to her efforts and the saving grace of Jesus.

Huldah's and Mother Teresa's missions are right down the street from each other. While in town, we visited both. Huldah shared that Mother Teresa had told her, "It's not how much you do that counts, it's how much love you put into what you do."

On the several occasions we have spent time with Huldah, she frequently remarks on how much she feels she hasn't done enough. Amazing. She has done more than many of us will ever dream to do, and yet she longs for justice for more and more people. Even after all that has been accomplished, she still feels the inadequacies of her own humanity and sees the great needs left in Calcutta and the nation of India. I believe this is common to all of us. Don't keep score, just get to work, and allow God to use you. What God can do with one life fully committed to him for a lifetime of bringing justice to the poor is mind-boggling.

Let's Not Take Justice for Granted

Sometimes we take organizations that are doing so much good for granted. Organizations like Convoy of Hope, Samaritan's Purse, and the Red Cross provide relief on the ground after a devastating flood or hurricane. It is important that we join with the efforts already happening. Some people wonder if their donation will get lost in a large organization, but most well-known organizations have their percentages listed on charity websites. The majority of each gift goes directly to meet real needs. Let's be more supportive and continue our legacy in America of being the most generous nation on earth. God has blessed us so much—let's bless as many other people as we can by bringing justice and helping the poor.

Go to www.thinke.org for Challenge #5.

To Think About

1. What story speaks the most to you and why does it grip your heart?

2. Have you been involved with feeding the hungry or serving the poor? How did this experience affect you?

3. Hearing the stories of those in need, how can you be more grateful for the many blessings God has put in your life?

4. What organizations do you know of that are helping people? How can you support and partner with them in greater ways?

Notes

[1] Scott Noble, "The Future of America – and Christianity," *Christian Examiner*, Minnesota edition (out of print), December 2012. Used with permission of author. Italics mine.

[2] Website of End It Movement, http://enditmovement.com/#together_we_can.

[3] Lynne Hybels, "Syrian Refugees, Wardrobe Enhancement, and 2014," *Lynne Hybels* (blog), January 12, 2014, http://lynnehybels.blogspot.com/2014/01/syrian-refugees-wardrobe-enhancement_12.html.

[4] Lynne Hybels, March 8, 2014, accessed October 27, 2014, https://twitter.com/lynnehybels/status/442280725144809472.

Chapter Six

TO THE ENDS OF THE EARTH (MISSIONAL MOVEMENTS)

*The gospel is bearing fruit and growing
throughout the whole world—just as it has
been doing among you since the day you
heard it and truly understood God's grace.*

—Colossians 1:6

In 2013, I traveled to Philadelphia, part of the historical center of our nation, with Greg Laurie and the Harvest America team. I had admired Greg's ministry and passion for the Lord over the years, and it's been such a privilege to partner with them in recent years. Greg is a pastor of a very large church in Southern California. He came to Christ during the Jesus movement, and the Calvary Chapel has been a significant part of his faith journey.

Greg was born out of wedlock in the 1950s; his mom was married and divorced seven times. Through no fault of his own, he grew up in an environment of alcohol abuse, pain, and mistrust. Growing up as a child of the 1960s, he soon turned to parties and drinking. Greg shares: "Some people say sin is fun, and that's true to a degree, but that's only for a short, short season. And all that's left is just a dull ache."[1] In the summer of his senior year of high school, he heard words he had never heard before: there was someone who loved him, someone who would never leave him, and someone he could trust. That day, he chose to follow Jesus.

Over forty years later, he now has shared the gospel with millions of people in stadiums across the nation, over radio, on TV, and through the Internet. Harvest America has been a campaign over the past several years that allows local churches across the nation to simulcast a live outreach event with Greg and popular music artists. I had the privilege of standing just a few feet from the stage as Greg shared the gospel in Philadelphia with audiences of tens of thousands of people in person, and an additional audience of hundreds of thousands on the simulcast in four thousand venues across the nation. The presence of God was palpable, and the stage floor at Wells Fargo Center rumbled as thousands walked down the aisles to publicly profess that they wanted to trust in Jesus's finished work on the cross for them. Nearly thirty thousand people have made decisions for Christ through Harvest America in two years. If this is what is going on through one event, and a single ministry, can you imagine what is happening through the countless efforts of God's people all over the world? There is far more going on than we will ever realize.

Christianity Is Growing at Three Times the Rate of the World's Population

People are coming to faith in Christ at a rate like no other time in human history, especially in the global South. When my older brother Jon was in Bogotá, Columbia, a decade ago, he attended a church with a quarter million weekly attendees and a weekly youth group service with seventy thousand young people meeting in a soccer stadium. The pastor there shared, "Christianity is growing at three times the rate of the world's population. In America only is it decreasing."

But even this quote can be deceiving, since America still has the number one population of Christians in the world. In fact, *ten times more Americans attend church on a single weekend than the crowds that fill all the NFL football stadiums over the entire football season.*[2] We see the massive crowds surging into stadiums and creating road-blocking traffic jams, but we should note that this is a drop in the bucket compared to the movement in the kingdom of God in America. And it's really not about being bigger or better than anyone, it's simply a reminder that God is at work in surprising ways in surprising amounts of people all around us.

It's not hard for me to believe these numbers anymore. In the past decade, God has blessed me with the opportunity to meet many influential evangelistic leaders who've individually led millions of people to faith in Christ. *I'm not sure we could say this about George Whitfield, Jonathan Edwards, Charles Finney, or John Wesley, but we can say it about various leaders today.* I'm not saying this to downplay what they saw in their day, but rather to simply encourage believers in what God is doing in our day. I've had the great privilege of meeting and spending moments with Franklin Graham, the son of Billy Graham and president of the Billy Graham Evangelistic Association; Greg Laurie of Harvest Crusades; Luis Palau of the Luis Palau Festivals, which have drawn crowds of hundreds of thousands to single citywide festivals; Carlos Annacondia, who has led millions to faith in Christ across Argentina; Vonnette Bright who, along with her husband Bill, launched the Cru Movement, the Jesus Film Project, and the Four Spiritual Laws; Loren Cunningham, who launched a worldwide missions movement through YWAM, which has discipled millions; and other leaders who've had a similar impact.

Truly, there are influential leaders in all the nations of the earth that we haven't heard of, but who are having significant impact in reaching their nations with the gospel. Two friends of mine have had the opportunity to speak for the Winter Jam Tour over the past decade, along with NewSong and Johnny Hunt of the Southern Baptist denomination, and they have watched with their own eyes in just the past few years as hundreds of thousands of young people in America have made decisions for Christ. The list could go on and on. It never ceases to amaze me how active God is in other people's lives, and how many people these days are open and responding to the message of Jesus.

What Is the Meaning of Life?

In addition to individuals preaching the gospel, there are many movements that are resulting in people finding and following Jesus. The Alpha Course has been highly influential in leading millions of people to Christ all over the world. Run by Nicky Gumbel out of Holy Trinity Brompton in London, Alpha comes alongside local churches to create an environment where it is safe to ask questions about the faith and try to understand the truth of the gospel. This has created a groundswell all over the world. In churches, and at times even in coffee shops, homes, and bars, twenty-two million people have participated in the Alpha Course in 169 countries since its inception.

Alpha has done its best to create an environment where people can get their questions answered about faith in Jesus. It is promoted to seekers with billboards and flyers like "What is the meaning of life?" "Do you believe in God?" and "Is there more to life than this?" For some time, one of the promoters of the course was Bear Grylls, who is well known for his TV series *Man vs. Wild*.

Gospel Movements in America

Christian leaders in America have not only been proclaiming the gospel of Jesus, but they have also been more and more thoughtful in their approach. Christians are a massive movement that can be mobilized for good, more than any other institution in society.

Kevin Palau, the oldest son of Luis Palau and president of the Palau Association, has been on the forefront of encouraging church leaders across America to think of the ways they can serve and add value to their city. Events are great, powerful, and often God-ordained, but a unified citywide effort can often go further in its scope and impact to better the city that we live in. Kevin defines a gospel movement as "a united, sustainable effort by churches and cultural leaders to transform their city by meeting critical needs and sharing the love and message of Jesus Christ."[3]

Kevin and the Palau Association have been utilizing this model in recent years, and it has brought them to working alongside the openly gay mayor of Portland, Oregon. They have found ways they can work alongside the city and important needs they can all agree on—like solving the issue of human trafficking in their city. All this has dramatically increased the effectiveness of their outreaches in that area as the gospel is proclaimed; but just as important, they have served their city without an agenda, with the brilliant love of Jesus Christ. Their story is inspiring and worth your time to look up and watch at CityServePDX.org.

A group of churches in the Twin Cities took a step like this last year and canceled their Sunday services one weekend a year to get out and serve their communities' felt needs. Something about this speaks volumes to those outside the church—that we do not simply want to be a holy huddle, but we care about serving people. This is an idea other groups of churches in other cities need to pick up and run with as well.

China on Course to Surpass America as Nation with Most Christians

This headline encourages me in so many ways—firstly because it is so far beyond my paradigm of what God is doing in the other parts of the world.

The Global Network of Mission Structures told us in 2010, "Today, there are over 4,000 known evangelical mission agencies sending out 250,000 missionaries from over 200 countries. This is up from 1,800 known mission agencies and 70,000 missionaries in 1980."[4] And then Melissa Steffan came along and pointed out, similar to the above paradigm-shifting title, "The country that received the most missionaries in 2010? The United States, with 32,400 sent from other nations."[5]

The second reason this fact encourages me is that my great-great-great-uncle Henry J. Brown was the first Mennonite missionary to China in the early 1900s.

There's a great TV show called *Who Do You Think You Are?* that follows celebrities as they discover their genealogy and ancestry roots. I'm not sure if you have ever looked into your past, but there is something so powerful about learning about your ancestors. From my Italian Pentecostal ancestors on my Grandma Brown's side, who used to pray for future generations to be used by God, to my wife's great-relative who was ordained by John Wesley, founder of the Methodists, I always love learning about my ancestors, especially their spirituality.

Only in the past year did I learn about Henry J. Brown from my parents. Interestingly, he wrote several books about his experiences as a missionary that I'm told were very popular in Mennonite circles, although they are out of print and unavailable on platforms like Amazon today. Thankfully, his son is still alive, after himself spending a lifetime of medical missions in China. My dad wrote to him, and he found a few copies of his dad's books for us. The one I have is one of my most treasured possessions. It is such a privilege to read his spiritual wisdom and learn from his experiences. Amazingly, although he was raised in Missouri, he traveled and preached as an itinerant evangelist in Minnesota for a time. Now, one hundred years later, I'm sure I've traveled some of the same roads across the state to speak of Christ to the same communities.

He became the very first missionary to China for the General Conference Mennonite Church, a group of Anabaptist Mennonites. He spent the majority of his life as a missionary there (and later, his son did as well). He initially went without the formal support of his denomination in 1909, because the call was too strong. It wasn't until 1914 that he was officially endorsed by his denomination. How encouraging it is to read his riveting, faith-filled stories of God coming through and doing miracles to sustain his missionary endeavors. His faith gives me faith that God will come through for us.

Henry Brown spent several years in a Chinese prison for spreading the gospel. After some time back in the United States, his family eventually returned to China, where they had previously been imprisoned, to continue their work. They were part of the generation of missionaries responsible for the underground church and staggering growth of Christianity across the nation today. It seems that he was a godly, effective, and wise leader.

According to their records, "He proposed a plan to share leadership of the church and mission with the Chinese Christians." I'm so grateful for the godly heritage we appreciate today, and it is my heart's desire that we in turn leave this same kind of legacy of prayer, faith, and obedience for generations yet to come. I hope you feel the same.

On to what's happening in China one hundred years after my uncle Henry. Joe Carter, who writes for the *The Gospel Coalition*, reported:

> The number of Christians in Communist China is growing so steadily that by 2030 it could have more churchgoers than America.
>
> The People's Republic of China remains, at least officially, an atheist country. But the number of Protestant Christians in China has grown from one million in 1949 to more than 49 million in 2010. Experts believe that number could more than triple over the next generation. . . .
>
> Sociologist Rodney Stark estimates that during the first 350 years of Christianity, the faith grew at a rate of 40 percent per decade. During the 61-year period from 1949 to 2010, Christianity grew at a rate of 4,800 percent in 61 years, a rate of 89% per decade. . . .
>
> By mid-century, China may have more citizens who identify as Christians than the United States has citizens.
>
> Christians in America often find reasons to be pessimistic about our religion's waning influence on our country. But we should remember that our land is

not the last bastion of hope for the faith. The remarkable growth in global Christianity—particularly in Asia and Africa—should give us reason to be optimistic. The Holy Spirit is changing hearts and minds around the globe in a way that has not been seen since the first century after Christ's Ascension. For this we should be eternally grateful.[6]

Just think of it! On the other end of the globe, God is at work in millions upon millions of people's lives. No matter whether emperors, kings, or presidents make Christianity illegal or uncomfortable, the kingdom of God continues to capture the hearts and minds of people everywhere (sometimes, like we see in China, especially in those parts of the world that try to stop it) because it is a work of the Holy Spirit, which cannot be stopped. Paul said: "Because I preach this Good News, I am suffering and have been chained like a criminal. But the word of God cannot be chained" (2 Tim. 2:9 NLT).

The Muslim World Is Trusting Christ in Surprising Numbers

Not only in China, but also in other parts of the world, where even calling yourself a Christian could cause your life to be at risk, God is working by his Spirit to raise to preeminence the gospel of his Son, Jesus.

I had the privilege of speaking recently with Naghmeh Abedini, whose husband, Saeed, is currently imprisoned in Iran. Although he is an American citizen, his life is in grave danger for preaching the gospel and working with churches in Iran. She is working hard, with many people supporting her, to seek freedom for him. It should not be overlooked that because of this situation, God has opened doors for her to preach the gospel to the delegates of the United Nations,[7] as well as on television to millions across Iran. Only God could take something so devastating and use it for so much good. We all need to join with her in calling for his release and the release of other Christians wrongly imprisoned for their faith in Jesus Christ. It is important for us to "remember those in prison as if you were together with them in prison, and those who are mistreated as if you yourselves were suffering" (Heb. 13:3).

On other parts of the middle east, *Christianity Today* reports (italics mine):

> After traveling 250,000 miles through Dar al-Islam ("House of Islam") as Muslims call their world, career missiologist David Garrison came to a startling conclusion: Muslim background believers are leading Muslims to Christ in staggering numbers, but not in the West. *They are doing this primarily in Muslim-majority nations almost completely under the radar—of everyone. . . .*
>
> - In Algeria, after 100,000 died in Muslim-on-Muslim violence, 10,000 Muslims turned their backs on Islam and were baptized as followers of Christ. This movement has tripled since the late 1990s.
> - At the time of the 1979 revolution in Iran, about 500 individual Muslims were following Christ. Garrison projects that today there may be several hundred thousand Christ-followers, mostly worshipping in Iranian house churches.
> - In an unnamed Arab nation, an Islamic book publisher Nasr came to Christ through satellite

broadcast evangelist Father Zakaria. Sensing a call to evangelize, Nasr started a local ministry that in less than one year baptized 2,800 individuals.

In total, Garrison estimates that 2 to 7 million people from a Muslim background worldwide now follow Christ.[8]

Catholicism and the New Pope

Let's do another quiz—guess who said this quote? "When we walk without the cross, when we build without the cross and when we proclaim Christ without the cross, we are not disciples of the Lord. We are worldly."[9] That would be the new Pope, Pope Francis. If you've had a chance to hear some of the news surrounding the new Pope Francis, you are probably amazed, encouraged, and stirred by what God might continue to do in the Catholic church around the world.

While I don't intend to take on the entire subject of Catholics and Christians, I want to express my support and great desire to see Catholics everywhere as brothers and sisters in Christ. For hundreds of years now, relations between Catholic and Protestant Christians have been a struggle. I do believe, very much, that the Reformation was absolutely necessary. Any time a denomination within Christianity denies the clear guidance of Scripture, they are absolutely wrong. The apostle Paul said, "But even if we or an angel from heaven should preach a gospel other than the one we preached to you, let them be under God's curse!" (Gal. 1:8). Paul does not give an exemption . . . not even for himself! It is the true gospel or nothing at all. It doesn't matter how big a Christian leader or denomination is; if they deny the clear truth of Scripture, they are dead wrong. Since the Reformation, both Catholics and Protestants have denied the other's salvation and credibility many times. But I believe this is slowly changing. *If we can agree that faith in Jesus is the foundation of our faith, and put our trust in him alone, we are on the same hallowed ground together before the cross.* Is every person who calls themselves a Catholic a true Christian? Definitely not. But then again, neither is every Baptist person, or charismatic person. This aside, I have met many Catholic believers who have true saving faith in Jesus Christ. And I believe this tide is rising.

It breaks my heart that we so quickly and harshly want to excommunicate a billion people who claim to put their trust in Christ. I've read over a hundred books on church history, and in all my study of church history—including the earliest church histories known to us today—*leaders have continually prayed and called out that the church might be of one heart.*

This was likewise one of Jesus's final recorded prayers with his disciples before going to the cross:

> I pray that they will all be one, just as you and I are one—as you are in me, Father, and I am in you. And may they be in us so that the world will believe you sent me. I have given them the glory you gave me, so they may be one as we are one. I am in them and you are in me. May they experience such perfect unity that the world will know that you sent me and that you love them as much as you love me. (John 17:21–23 NLT)

Jesus isn't necessarily calling us to cancel out all denominations and join the Catholic Church, or Protestant Church, or Evangelical Church, or Pentecostal Church, or Reformed Church. *He is calling us to love each other in spite of the name of the denomination over our door. If we believe in his love, and we follow his teachings, we are brothers and sisters of the same Father in heaven.* We need to work at being more gracious to each other. We need to pray for each other. We need to stop trying to "kick each other out of the boat" when we disagree on nonessential theology. We need to do a better job understanding each other and giving grace. A good question might be: Are we known more for our disagreements or our love?

It's not that denominations need to agree on everything, but let's just remember we are one family living to bring glory to Jesus, and cheer each other on. *Let's all agree to focus less on being Catholic, Reformed, Pentecostal, or Evangelical, and more on being a Christian.* Let's focus less on what divides us and more on what unites us. We are a part of something bigger than our sectarian theologies, no matter how narrow some leaders try to make them.

Obviously, there will be important issues on which we disagree. The main difference is: *Don't reject Christians who are different than you. Instead, reel them in to a more full understanding of the gospel.* This is the example the apostle Paul set for us in Acts, chapter 19.

It's amazing to me that many Christians will quote Ghandi or Mark Twain, but they would never quote a pastor down the street with a slightly different theology than they have. We know we do not grasp the glory of the gospel if we get more excited about all our side theology than over the fact of Christ crucified and raised from the dead. Christ is first, and everything else is secondary. Let's build our lives on him. We are often too quick to dishonor other Christians who are different than we are, and cry heresy toward anyone who would seek unity among people who trust in Jesus.

We too quickly forget that we all started out Catholic. Every Christian's roots go back to the godly leaders through the centuries that based out of the Catholic church. We are too quick to disown our own "bloodline" of the faith, even though Jesus shed his blood that we would be one.

Philip Jenkins, professor of religion at Pennsylvania State University and prolific author, writes in his groundbreaking books *The Next Christendom* and *The Lost History of Christianity* about how much more diverse the Christian world has been than we ever realized, and how diverse it is increasingly becoming. He also suggests how important it is that our faith reaches across diverse spectrums of society, and that all the parts don't look exactly like each other. He writes,

> Churches succeed when they reach broadly across sections of society and make their religion part of the ordinary lived reality of a diverse range of communities. They also survive best when they diversify in global terms, so they are not dependent on just one region of the world, however significant that region might appear at a given time.[10]

What Jenkins as a historian and sociologist suggests to keep Christianity from tapering off, we see as God's great desire for every nation and people on earth. God doesn't want to keep people out of his kingdom. He gave everything in his Son Jesus to get them in. Let's do the same.

Evangelism Has Become a Dirty Word

So how does all this affect or inspire you, personally? Are you going to go preach to crowds? Likely, not many of us will stand before thousands to testify to the gospel, although some of us may. But God asks all of us to radiate his goodness and light in our lives to the people around us.

Perhaps one of the greatest hindrances to the American church sharing the love of Christ is that evangelism is viewed so poorly these days. A friend called it the "E-word" while we were talking about a church event he was putting on. It was focused on helping Christians share their faith in Jesus—evangelism. In a true sense, talking about faith has become a bad word for many Americans. The two things we are told never to talk about are religion and politics.

Michelle and I ran into an evangelist in San Francisco two years back. If you've never been to San Fran, it is quite a treat. Michelle and I flew in for work in the fall, and we spent a few days traveling up and down the Pacific Coast Highway—U.S. Highway 1. Michelle and I picked up a rental car at the airport and found out that in California you can pick out whatever car model you want, so we went with a bright red Dodge Challenger. I felt so cool driving it all weekend long. We whisked along the winding roads, heading south away from the city, to a small, delightful town called Carmel by the Sea. We grabbed a quick bite at an Italian restaurant, and by the stares we were getting, I'm pretty sure we were underdressed . . . it's kind of a fancy little town. The next day, we walked from our hotel over to the convention center where we were working during the Oracle Conference. I noticed a short, stocky gentleman on the street corner in the midst of all the passersby and the hustle and bustle of a large conference (an estimated thirty thousand people were in attendance that year).

Suddenly, the man on the street corner began to scream! It was not your average yip or yell; this was a high-pitched, throaty kind of scream that you'd assume would cause just about anyone to lose his voice within a few minutes of unleashing it. He began to wave his Bible back and forth in the air, and from the small bits and bumbles I could make out between his gasps for breath and relief for his throat, I could tell he was saying something about Jesus . . . and repentance . . . and God. Passersby quickly skirted him and crossed the street as fast as they could, and I can only imagine them adding one more entry to their list of reasons not to use the E-word.

As I've gone back over this experience, and also reminisced about how much I want to go back and visit San Francisco with Michelle, my main deduction is that this stocky street preacher was using the wrong bait. Jesus talked to his first followers about "fishing for men." I'm not much of a fisherman myself, aside from the occasional sunny day (we have ten thousand lakes in Minnesota, so it's almost a sin not to do all that fun lake stuff). If fishing has anything to do with the E-word, we can easily assume that different bait works for different people; and it is easy to see that screaming at a person (or thirty thousand of them) is going to be among the most unsuccessful bait possible.

A girl named Addie wrote recently about the E-word:

[Campus Crusade for Christ] was hugely significant in my mom's life. It was through them that she
discovered the depths of God's love for her and was
changed by it. It's a unique piece of my spiritual heritage, one that I haven't spent much time thinking
about or exploring. In my post-Super-Christian life, I
have found that I have a sort of a knee-jerk reaction to
words like "witness" and "evangelize." They instantly
raise my stress level and my defenses, and I'm not
sure how to navigate the choppy waters of speaking

> my faith out loud anymore. Still, the fact remains:
> my mom knows this Love because someone told
> her about it. And for me, a generation later, that fact
> changed everything.[11]

I love that. All I know is that while evangelism has become a dirty word, I want to believe God can do something different with it through my life and your life . . . if we can only focus on caring about people more authentically and loving people more unconditionally, and if we don't scream at them.

We have to put ourselves in the apostles' shoes. When they traveled with Jesus, what did they say? What did they do? I've done my fair share of street evangelism. It took me many years to realize something profound: the first followers of Jesus did not witness to every person they met on the street. In my mind, I had somehow come to the conclusion that the more we witness to strangers, the holier we become. I used to think if I could just witness to literally every person I came into contact with throughout my day, I would have made it into kingdom greatness. (I seriously thought this.)

It took some time and some years for me to understand Acts 17:2: "As was his custom, Paul went into the synagogue, and on three Sabbath days he reasoned with them from the Scriptures." What did Paul do on the days in between? We don't exactly know, but we see that on every church day he took opportunities to speak of Christ, proclaim Christ, and call men and women to Christ. Paul wasn't rabidly evangelizing every single person he met throughout the week (although he did personal evangelism at times), yet we can still see the spread of the gospel was the driving force of his life.

The gospel frees us from the notion that the evangelization of the world falls on our shoulders alone. I believe in reaching the world. I believe that God has placed each of us in the time we live in, growing up where we grow up for a reason (see Acts 17:26–28). But it is God alone who draws men and women to himself (John 6:44), and it is the church collectively that is called to reach the world. Not me alone—the church together—with every part working its unique strength (Eph. 4:16) that God can use for his glory.

We can play a small part in God's grand story: the rescue and redemption of the world. Our role is led by the Spirit and focused on Christ. We carry it out by setting apart Christ as Lord within our own hearts, giving an answer to anyone who asks for the hope we have received, and always sharing of Christ with gentleness and respect for our hearers (1 Pet. 3:15). Our role is to be faithful to the leadings and promptings of the Holy Spirit in the large and small stages of our lives. If we are to "do the work of the evangelist," we must study the life of Christ and also the story of Philip the Evangelist in Acts 8. He was led at key moments by the Spirit: where to go, what to do, what to say. He was prepared with a proper understanding of the Word of God and how to point a seeker toward Jesus.

Evangelism becomes a dirty word when it is done religiously out of human motivation (often guilt and aiming to earn God's pleasure through works) and attempted through human strength. The antidote comes from understanding our proper role as simple tools in the hands of God. "Neither the one who plants nor the one who waters is anything, but only God, who makes things grow. The one who plants and the one who waters have one purpose, and they will each be rewarded according to their own labor." (1 Cor. 3:7–8)

The message of evangelism is not just "go," but also "I am with you always" (see Matt. 28:19-21). It is Christ's presence that heals. It is Christ's presence that saves. It is Christ's presence that delivers. We are needy of his presence every day in every way. Unless God moves and does through us what he loves to do best, hearts will remain darkened to the light of the gospel.

The Modesto Manifesto

The good news is that we don't have to leave evangelism as a dirty word. We can redefine what God has meant evangelism to be and change people's minds one at a time.

I love this old story of Billy Graham and his close friends from half a century ago—it is just as relevant for us today. It was 1949, and Graham and his team were struggling with the perceptions of evangelism in their day.

> Billy instructed all of us, "Boys, let's go to our rooms and write down all of the criticisms of mass evangelism. Don't hold anything back. Then, let's meet for evaluation and prayer this afternoon."
>
> All of us agreed that our number-one pet peeve was the handling of finances. We also listed sensationalism, over-emotionalism, becoming controversial, and the image of being anti-intellectual and anti-church. And there was the matter of virtually no follow-up.
>
> That very day we determined not to be guilty of those charges, and the Team set out to make necessary changes and adjustments. . . . We had determined at our Modesto prayer meeting to "abstain from all appearance of evil" (1 Thessalonians 5:22).

Through careful planning and perspiration, under the leadership of the Spirit, we set out to live down the stereotypes of evangelism.[12]

When we do this, when we live down the stereotypes of evangelism and pursue the heart of God—which is for people—we can see life change happen. People matter to God, so people should matter to us. We should do what we need to do to make the gospel clear and compelling to them. My friend Pradeepan, who comes from a Sri Lankan Hindu background, shared how he came to faith in Jesus because he was invited to a church service where young people were excited about God and passionate about life: "Seeing people in the house of God, filled with true life and love, moved me to the point of salvation. I asked questions about God because I felt exposed to a new way of life." He went on to explain, *"If we show people Christians are better than they had believed, they might start to think God is better than they had believed."*

This is also how the late Bill Bright, founder of Campus Crusade for Christ (now known as Cru), came to faith in Christ. In Southern California, he was pursuing the everyman's dream in life, success and wealth, until he came across some young, passionate Christians who were full of God's love and life, and this drew him to the point of salvation. He went on to spend his life reaching millions with the gospel. More than anything else, people need to see us enjoying a rich, satisfying relationship with Christ.

As Simple as One, Two . . . Four

A relative started attending a new church and shared excitement about the vision of the pastor that, together, their church of a few thousand could reach seven hundred thousand people with the gospel in the next ten years. Numbers like that sound elusive, but they are far easier and simpler to reach than any of us would dare believe—especially with the help of the Holy Spirit.

Don Osman explains the power of simply pointing one person at time to the goodness of Jesus.

> If I were a big-time evangelist and every year I led 30,000 people to Christ, over a 22 year period, I would have led 660,000 people to Christ. But if I decided as a strategic evangelist to reach one unsaved person and disciple that one person so that he or she would reach another person, over a 22 year period, through a multiplication process, I would have reached about 1.04 million people.[13]

The impact we can all have by simply obeying the simple words of Jesus is astounding.

As you can see, if we are all a bit more intentional, and take our efforts deeper into relationship with people, we can make a huge difference in our generation. So let's all agree to join in the great movement of God in helping people see the same awakening we have experienced in our own hearts and lives.

Go to www.thinke.org for Challenge #6.

To Think About

1. How do you see faith in America today? Where do you see signs of hope?

2. Have you ever shared your faith in Christ? How did the person you were sharing with receive it?

3. What does it mean to you that Christianity is growing all over the world? How does this encourage your faith?

4. How can you see other Christians in a better light, instead of casting them off as less-than-believers? Is there anything you need to repent of in this area?

Notes

[1] Greg Laurie, "A Short Biography of Greg Laurie," Harvest Christian Fellowship video posted on YouTube, August 13, 2011, www.youtube.com/ watch?v=1nJwoAGt2Yo.

[2] An estimated 40 percent of Americans attend church on any given weekend according to most research, which equals 125 million people. (Source: http://thegospelcoalition.org/blogs/justintaylor/2007/03/01/ how-many-americans-attend-church-each.) Fewer than 17 million people attend NFL football games through the entire season, according to online sources. (Source: http://profootballtalk.nbcsports.com/2012/07/08/ after-peaking-in-2007-nfl-attendance-steadily-has-declined.)

[3] About page for Gospel Movement, http://gospelmovements.org/about.

[4] Global Network of Mission Structures, "Acceleration the Fulfillment of the Great Commission in our Generation," *GNMS*, 2010, accessed October 27, 2014, http://www.gnms.net/envisioning.html.

[5] Melissa Steffan, "The Surprising Countries Most Missionaries Are Sent From and Go To," *Christianity Today*, July 25, 2013, accessed October 27, 2014, http://www.christianitytoday.com/gleanings/2013/july/missionaries-countries-sent-received-csgc-gordon-conwell.html.

[6] Joe Carter, "China On Course to Become 'World's Most Christian Nation,'" *The Gospel Coalition*, April 21, 2014, http://thegospelcoalition.org/blogs/tgc/2014/04/21/ china-on-course-to-become-worlds-most-christian-nation.

[7] This video of Naghmeh sharing at the United Nations is available for watching on YouTube at http://www.youtube.com/ watch?v=o3TGCtMTQg4.

[8] Timothy Morgan, "Why Muslims Are Becoming the Best Evangelists," *Christianity Today*, April 22, 2014, www.christianitytoday.com/ct/2014/ april-web-only/why-muslims-are-becoming-best-evangelists.html. (This is a projection since a comprehensive count is not possible.)

[9] Crispian Balmer and Philip Pullella, "New Pope Urges Church to Return to Its Gospel Roots, *Reuters*, March 14, 2013, www.reuters.com/ article/2013/03/14/us-pope-idUSBRE92D05P20130314.

[10] Philip Jenkins, *The Lost History of Christianity* (New York: HarperOne, 2008), 244.

[11] Addie Zierman, "Witness-Wear," *Addie Zierman* (blog), May 15, 2012, http://addiezierman.com/2012/05/15/witness-wear.

[12] Grady Wilson, *Count It All Joy* (Nashville: Broadman Press, 1984), 46, 50.

[13] Don Osman, *The Mission of An Evangelist* (Minneapolis: World Wide Publications, 2001.), 277–278.

Chapter Seven

THE END GOAL
(GLORY OF GOD)

There is not a square inch in the whole domain of our human existence over which Christ, who is Sovereign over all, does not cry, "Mine!"

—Abraham Kuyper

In 2012, in the south metro of the Twin Cities in Minnesota, Bethany International hosted a conference with Loren Cunningham, founder of Youth With A Mission. I have followed Loren's writings and ministry for years, and I jumped at the chance to spend time with and learn from one of my heroes of the faith. Youth With A Mission, known to many simply as YWAM, has nearly one million Discipleship Training School alumni, and over five million alumni have gone through their various ministries over the past six decades since it was launched in the mid-twentieth century.

I had the honor of hosting a radio interview with Loren before the conference, and I sat in various meetings at the conference as he shared. In one of the meetings, Loren shared firsthand about an encounter he had with Bill Bright, founder of Campus Crusade for Christ, a few decades earlier.

In 1975, Bill Bright and Loren Cunningham ran into each other at the Denver airport and decided to grab lunch together. Loren excitedly began to tell Bill about a recent vision God had given him. In the middle of his sharing, Bill pulled a scribbled-on piece of paper out of his bag with his notes on the exact same vision God had given him! The vision was "if we are to impact any nation for Jesus Christ, we would have to affect the seven spheres, or mountains of society that are the pillars of any society." The "seven mountains" the Lord showed both of them the church needed to scale, were business, government, media, arts and entertainment, family, and religion. "It was here where culture would be won or lost."[1] God was showing them that ministry is more than just at church, and to truly influence culture, we need to take the gospel into every sphere of society, and inspire others to do this as well.

Occupy All Streets

In 2013, Hillsong NYC (part of the Hillsong Church in Australia) highlighted a series based on the "Occupy Wall Street" movement, and coined the phrase "Occupy All Streets." This is what it means for the church to occupy all streets—not simply to occupy seats within a church, but to occupy streets across the earth. I don't necessarily mean we need to embark on an aggressive form of street evangelism, but rather to take our personal experience with the goodness and glory of God and let it shine in the places he has called each of us to, whether that is a bank, medical research facility, scientific lab, investment firm, foreign nation, or beyond.

And it's important that we know it is not about our role. Our heroes in Scripture were not all preachers or pastors. We need simply to walk closely with the Lord, to see and behold his glory for ourselves, to do exactly what he tells us to do, and then to take the message of his goodness to whatever corner of the world he places us in.

One surprising example of Christians taking their place and showing excellence in all areas of society is highlighted in an article from *Christianity Today*:

> The media often portrays scientists and Christians as incapable of peaceful coexistence. But results from a recent survey suggest the two are not as incompatible as one might think. In fact, 2 million out of nearly 12 million scientists are evangelical Christians. If you were to bring all the evangelical scientists together, they could populate the city of Houston, Texas.[2]

In fact, the study by sociologist Elaine Howard Ecklund, her colleagues at Rice University, and the American Association for the Advancement of Science shows that 61 percent of all scientists in the United States are professing Christians. This compared to 24.4 percent who are professing atheists. "The survey also found that evangelical scientists are more active in their faith than American evangelicals in general. They are more likely to consider themselves very religious, to attend religious services weekly, and to read religious texts at least every week."[3]

And isn't this how it should be? Christians shouldn't relegate themselves to "holier" professions. They should follow the leading of God on their life—which leads them into all areas of society. They should work to represent God well there: "Whatever you do, work at it with all your heart, as working for the Lord, not for human masters, since you know that you will receive an inheritance from the Lord as a reward. It is the Lord Christ you are serving" (Col. 3:23–24).

Abraham Kuyper reminds us, "There is not a square inch in the whole domain of our human existence over which Christ, who is Sovereign over all, does not cry, 'Mine!'" This message of Christ's glory must also be evident outside the church walls and spill onto the streets of the earth.

And by *occupy*, I don't mean to take over in the sense that we are lifting up some earthly Christian form of government, and imposing Christian views and lifestyles on the rest of the population. Rather, we are called to represent Christ and his gospel through our love, our graciousness, and our humility. We are to sacrifice personal preferences and prefer others above ourselves—to truly care about people in our workplace, to truly care about our boss (wouldn't that be different than the world around us?). This is the kind of occupation Christ would have us bring about on the earth.

We represent Christ well at our job by doing our job well. If you are an artist, create great art. If you are a lawyer, represent clients with truth, integrity, and justice. If you are a preacher, faithfully disperse the truths of God to people and work every week to build your listeners up, not tear them down. If you are a photographer, capture light and lines to a depth that inspires those who see your work. We work with an uncommon diligence, and we care about those in our workplace with an authentic love. This gives us a platform to share the grace of Christ within us that enables our uncommon work.

We occupy in this way for one purpose, and one purpose only—that the glory of God would fill the earth, and that more and more people would experience and know this God of all glory.

Let the Whole Earth Be Filled with His Glory

This grace-occupying is not our ultimate mission. John Piper was right when he said, "Missions exists because worship doesn't."[4] Ultimately, we desire God to receive more and more glory, that more and more people would see and ascribe worth to God for all he has done. David cries out in his final prayer in Psalm 72: "Let the whole earth be filled with his glory!" This is our prayer for our generation. But we also understand that in order for God to fill the earth with his glory, he has to fill us with his glory. In order for us to occupy all streets for the glory of God, the glory of God has to take up occupation in our own hearts.

God wants to fill the earth with his glory because his glory heals the earth. This is what every person on earth was created for. We were made for God. C. S. Lewis said: "If we find ourselves with a desire that nothing in this world can satisfy, the most probable explanation is that we were made for another world."[5] And every single one of us finds those unfulfilled desires within us. We were all made for God. We were all made chiefly to experience God's glory. We need God's grace and glory to fill our weary souls every day, every hour, every minute. Without it, we will never be satisfied. With it, we will never be the same.

Many Streams, One River

All these movements—prayer, justice, and evangelism—are for the express purpose of pointing back to God—pointing to his glory, his ultimate worth, and his goodness in the gospel, that we might worship him. Only in worshiping him are our souls truly satisfied and at rest. All these movements highlight Jesus, so that others might be drawn to him—the only name by which they can be saved. All these movements are really about one big God-story, about God's transforming reign in the nations of the earth. Habakkuk 2:14 gives us this enduring promise: "For the earth will be filled with the knowledge of the glory of the LORD as the waters cover the sea." This should be our prayer day after day and night after night.

Justice and evangelism are not separate aims or ends in and of themselves; they each flow into the singular, express purpose of every person who has encountered the glory of God—that the whole earth might experience his glory, just as the water covers the sea. It is all about Jesus.

To the extent that we tie our mission into this greater goal is the extent to which we will receive power and the wind of heaven blowing into the sails of our efforts. God wants to bless that which will point to the universe's ultimate purpose for being—to be filled with the glory of God just as the waters cover the sea; to be in all, to be through all, to be all. Christ is that all in all.

God in Pollsmoor Prison

My friend Dave Short, who oversees the Alpha Course on college campuses in the United States, shared some incredible thoughts in a blog post on our *Think Eternity* website:

> *For the vast majority of Americans, Jesus is "hid" from their sight, and the only plan Jesus gave us is one where we are responsible for making him visible.* I have had a lot of people over the years ask me why God doesn't just intervene more directly or make himself noticeable in a big way. Surely if God would "write something in the sky," or "appear in person to the world," people would turn to him.

However, in the Old Testament, God did take a more direct and active role in human history. The Exodus of the Israelites is a perfect example of God making some pretty dramatic appearances. However, as most of us are aware, these manifestations of God failed to produce lasting faith or change within people or culture. Since then, God has chosen to make himself known primarily through ordinary people like you and me. This means we have to provide evidence through our lives that Jesus is real to those from whom he is hidden.

Author Philip Yancey recalls a visit he had to South Africa in an interview with Alyson Quinn of Prison Fellowship:

> In South Africa I met a woman named Joanna—an ordinary, suburban woman. She and her husband had some education here in the U.S., and then they went back to South Africa. They were involved in the anti-apartheid movement, which was very successful. So she started praying. And the Lord's Prayer includes the phrase "thy kingdom come, thy will be done, on earth as it is in heaven." So she would pray, "Lord, show me a place where that's not true, where Your will is not being done on earth as it is in heaven, because we're supposed to be, as followers of You, part of the solution." Soon she found out that the most violent prison in South Africa, Pollsmoor Prison, was just minutes from her home. That year the prison recorded 279 acts of violence—almost one

a day! It was run by gangs. You would actually get points by stabbing somebody in another gang. If you stabbed a warden, you would get a lot of points. And it was severely overcrowded, as so many prisons are. And she thought, *Well, that's not right,* so she started going every day—365 days— she didn't skip Christmas or Easter, knowing those prisoners needed stability, something they could count on.

The year after she started going, there weren't 279 acts of violence in the prison. There were two. The BBC sent a camera crew from London to figure out what happened. . . . When I finally met with Joanna and her husband I said, "I think what you've done here is amazing. But tell me, what happened here? These guys are murderers; they're rapists; they're monsters. You just go in and act like a youth group and change the whole prison. What really happened?"

She looked at me, kind of shocked that I would ask such a question, and she said this line that I've repeated many places in the world because it so struck me. She said, "Well, of course, Philip, God was already present in Pollsmoor Prison. We just had to make him visible."[6]

In Genesis 28:16, it says, "When Jacob awoke from his sleep, he thought, 'Surely the LORD is in this place, and I was not aware of it.'" Many in our society are asleep to the reality of God and will only be made aware of him by our intentionality and involvement in their lives. Ordinary people like us are charged to make a loving God visible.[7]

As we allow God to shine through our diligence at work, in our care for others, and periodically as we speak of the gospel—his glory is then unveiled to more and more people. Daniel prophesied about us doing this when he said: "Those who are wise will shine like the brightness of the heavens, and those who lead many to righteousness, like the stars for ever and ever" (12:3). And we really can't do this by ourselves—we need God, by his Spirit, to show up and show off through our feeble attempts.

Bob Got the Bible to One Billion Children

Over the past half decade, I have had the privilege of working a bit each week with a Christian radio network in the Midwest, Praise FM. Praise FM has been in existence for twenty-nine years, and in the mid-nineties, God dramatically redirected the hearts of the executive director and the board to switch the format from Christian contemporary to worship. Ever since, they have been pioneering a new category in the radio industry, focused on worship. It is a fundamentally different way to do Christian radio, allowing moments for listeners to abide in Christ. Needless to say, this atmosphere of worship has been significant and beneficial to all aspects of their ministry endeavors. *There are certain ways to do ministry that are sticky to the presence and favor of God.* God seems especially to draw toward ministry efforts that are humble, focused on him, unifying believers from different backgrounds, built around the truth of the Word of God, proclaiming the gospel, and for the purpose of worship.

Through my time there, we have partnered with various nonprofits focused on getting the Word of God to children all over the world, stopping human trafficking, and feeding the poor in our own communities. It has been so encouraging to see what can happen when we come together. I also have been deeply influenced by the impact of Christian media. We must see discipleship as more than just an event or even a weekly one-hour church service. Discipleship must include more regular input, and Christian radio and social media are ways that we can go beyond the weekly service and be in people's lives during the daily grind, reminding them of the truth of Christ on Monday, not just on Sunday.

One of the nonprofits I've had the privilege of being around is OneHope, which is concentrating its efforts on getting the Word of God to every child in every nation. It is not slack in its vision, having recently brought the Word of God to its billionth child. This organization is also the producer of the Bible App for Kids, which was released with YouVersion's Bible App (you probably have this on your phone). Within weeks of being released, millions of families had downloaded the Bible App for Kids.

OneHope held a banquet this year celebrating their founder Bob Hoskins's seventy years of ministry, along with significant milestones in their ministry efforts. Possibly no one could share the story better than his son Rob:

> As a seven-year-old boy, my dad—Bob Hoskins— received a vision from the Lord, and preached his first sermon just days later. This year marks Dad's seventy amazing years doing God's work. . . .
>
> His evangelistic outreaches as a boy brought thousands to Christ. His missionary journeys as a teenager launched new churches. Mom and Dad raised us in

Lebanon, serving as missionaries in the Middle East.
After being evacuated because of war three times,
we moved and served in Europe planting seeds and
touching literally hundreds of thousands of lives with
the Good News.

OneHope was birthed out of yet another vision
God gave Dad; of Satan attacking the children of the
world and how desperately they needed to be rescued.
The rescue mechanism . . . would come in the form
of giving God's Word to every child . . . and it would
be done through leaders. Instead of shying away from
the giant task ahead, my dad said, "yes." . . .

Dad's legacy is "God's Word Every Child." And
under the banner, we've [now] reached more than a
billion children and youth with the Good News, all
around the world. . . .

On every continent, in nearly every nation, within
hundreds of people groups are children, families and
leaders that have received something lasting and eter-
nal from a man who dared to say "yes."[8]

Lauren Mcafee, a close friend of the Hoskins family, writes
about her personal experience attending the banquet for Bob
Hoskins: "I was amazed to think that because of one man's
faithfulness to the Lord . . . one billion children . . . have received
God's Word. What could God do with your life if you completely gave it to Him and faithfully followed his call?"[9]

I also appreciated the candid thoughts of Lauren's husband,
Michael. It captures the struggle we all have. We want to be
used by God, but we can easily find ourselves wanting to do it
for selfish reasons, rather than for God.

In the midst of [the banquet], I felt very . . . small.
Not in the way I should. I look at the men and the
missions that surrounded me and think "I need to be
doing MORE!" . . .

I want to have 70 years of faithful gospel ministry.
I don't want to waste my life. However, a lot of it was
my own pride. I saw men I admire and I want to be
an admired man. I saw godly men and women sharing stories of how God has used them to spread the
gospel and I think "I want to share a story like that so
that others might get to listen to ME." My motives
are so mixed.

God gave me this gift one day. He allowed me to
realize, this is a time for me to simply enjoy HIM and
to praise God for what He is accomplishing around
the world. . . .

Jesus wasn't calling me to work harder. Jesus was
calling me to worship better. . . . When my focus
is worship, I recognize that it is God who works
through me.[10]

Do you see yourself in this? Isn't this a struggle we all know too
well? In the midst of hearing about the great works of God, we
find ourselves wanting to experience the same, and it can often
turn into it being more about us than about God.

Let me ask you: What can God do with your life in the
next seventy years? Maybe you don't have that many left in
you, but what could he do in the next seven? If you truly said
yes to his call—if you lived your life as a sacrifice of worship
to him? Romans 12:1–2 reminds us: "Give your bodies to God
because of all he has done for you. Let them be a living and holy

sacrifice—the kind he will find acceptable. *This is truly the way to worship him.* Don't copy the behavior and customs of this world, but let God transform you into a new person by changing the way you think" (NLT; emphasis added). The median lifetime stretches for twenty-eight thousand days. Many of us may only have half that left. Don't you want to use every single day to say yes to God and his purposes for you? Let's allow God to iron out how he wants to use you as a sacrifice of worship.

Brennan Manning writes about his mentor Dominique, who was the leader of the Little Brothers of Jesus of the Franciscan order in Spain. Dominique writes in his final journal entry:

> All that is not the love of God has no meaning for me.
> I can truthfully say that I have no interest in anything
> but the love of God, which is in Christ Jesus. If God
> wants it to, my life will be useful through my word
> and witness. If He wants it to, my life will bear fruit
> through my prayers and sacrifices. But the usefulness
> of my life is His concern, not mine. It would be inde-
> cent of me to worry about that.[11]

We can get addicted to usefulness, but we need to be addicted to obedience as an act of worship. This is perhaps why God at times allows us to be stripped of opportunities and usefulness, and we are simply left with the most important work of all: worship. Go to www.thinke.org for Challenge #7.

To Think About

1. What story speaks the most to you and why does it grip your heart?

2. Have you viewed justice, evangelism, and prayer as separate aims? How do you see them now as one aim together for God's glory?

3. In what areas of your day-to-day activities can you work to "make God visible" to those around you?

4. How could God use your life over a lifetime to make a greater impact, as in Bob's story?

Notes

[1] Home page of Os Hillman's *7 Cultural Mountains*, www.7culturalmountains.org. For more on this, go to the full interview with Loren Cunningham: http://www.7culturalmountains.org/apps/articles/default.asp?articleid=40087&columnid=4347

Also, Loren Cunningham writes about this in his book *The Book That Transforms Nations* on pages 46–47.

[2] Christine Herman, "Study: 2 Million U.S. Scientists Identify as Evangelical," *Christianity Today*, February 20, 2014, accessed September 18, 2014, www.christianitytoday.com/ct/2014/february-web-only/study-2-million-scientists-identify-as-evangelical.html.

[3] Ibid.

[4] John Piper, *Let the Nations Be Glad*, 3rd edition (Ada, MI: Baker Academic, 2010), 15.

[5] C. S. Lewis, *Mere Christianity*, https://www.goodreads.com/quotes/6439-if-we-find-ourselves-with-a-desire-that-nothing-in.

[6] Philip Yancey interview with Alyson Quinn, *Prison Fellowship*, http://winterispast.blogspot.com/2011/09/how-to-make-god-visible-my-interview.html.

[7] Dave Short, "We Just Had to Make Him Visible," *Think Eternity* (blog), March 22, 2012, www.thinke.org/blog/2012/3/22/we-just-had-to-make-him-visible-by-dave-short.html.

[8] Rob Hoskins, "Legacy: Celebrating My Dad's 70th Year of Ministry," *Rob Hoskins* (blog), February 17, 2014, http://robhoskins.com/legacy-a-tribute-to-dad-as-we-celebrate-his-70th-year-of-ministry.

[9] Lauren McAfee, "OneHope Celebration," *Lauren Mcafee* (blog), February 19, 2014, http://laurenamcafee.com/2014/02/19/onehope-celebration.

[10] Michael McAfee, "Jesus Does Not Need You to Work Harder," *Michael McAfee* (blog), March 1, 2014, http://michaelmcafee.com/2014/03/01/jesusdoesnotneedyoutoworkharder.

[11] Brennan Manning, *All Is Grace* (Colorado Springs, CO: David C. Cook, 2011).

Section Three

LIVE INFLUENTIAL

Chapter Eight

LOOK WHAT HAS COME TO THE WORLD!

The early Christians did not exclaim, "What has the world come to?" Rather they proclaimed, "Look what has come to the world!"
—Carl F. H. Henry

Robert Cialdini shares a fascinating story in his book *Yes!* about the power of how we frame statements, and the effect it has on our listeners. This is important for Christians everywhere to understand. The Arizona State Petrified Forest National Park was having trouble with visitors taking pieces of petrified wood from the grounds, so they put up a sign stating, "Your heritage is being vandalized every day by theft losses of petrified wood of fourteen tons a year, mostly a small piece at a time." Little did they realize that although this statement was correct, "by using negative social proof as part of a rallying cry, they inadvertently focused the audience on the prevalence, rather than the undesirability of the behavior." Cialdini and his company became aware of the problem by a former graduate student.

He had visited the Petrified Forest with his
fiancée—a woman he described as the most honest
person he'd ever known, someone who had never bor-
rowed a paper clip without returning it. They quickly
encountered the aforementioned sign warning visitors against stealing petrified wood. He was shocked
when his otherwise wholly law abiding fiancée
nudged him in the side with her elbow and whispered,
"We'd better get ours now."

Cialdini and a team of others contacted the Park and set out to
test the concept of negative social proof. They created two signs
with the goal of deterring theft of the petrified wood. One used
negative social proof. Another sign didn't share any social proof,
stating "Please don't remove the wood from the park." They also
included a control condition in which they had no sign. "In a
finding that should petrify the National Park's management,
compared with a no-sign control condition in which 2.92 percent
of the pieces were stolen, the [negative] social proof message
resulted in *more* theft (7.92 percent). In essence, it almost tripled
theft. Thus, theirs was not a crime prevention strategy; it was a
crime *promotion* strategy." The second sign without social proof,
and even the control condition with no sign at all resulted in
significantly less theft, at 1.67 percent. "Simply reframing the
statistics can often do this. For example, although fourteen tons
of wood are stolen each year at the park, the actual number of
thieves is miniscule compared to the massive number of people
who respect the park."[1]

This story resonates with Christianity in America today.
The millennial generation is the largest and most unreached
generation in history. This should shock us, but we also need to

remember the majority of Americans still claim adherence to and faith in Jesus Christ. *It makes a big difference how you see and share the statistics.* Many generations of believers would've given anything to see what we get to be a part of today.

What We Talk about When We Talk about Christians in America

So many preachers and ministers could be to blame for the way the average Christian views the state of Christianity today. As a preacher myself, I know that we often have the "spiritual gift" of negativity. We talk about how our nation, our culture, and our community are going to hell in a handbasket. How many times have you heard a preacher say something like this? Or maybe I should ask: How many times have you heard a preacher *not* talk like this?

The problem, from the pulpit to the pew, is that we have framed so many of the statistics wrong. We have focused our local churches on the wrong things, and in trying to help, we have caused much harm. As Robert Cialdini explains, "by using negative social proof as part of a rallying cry, [we may] be inadvertently focusing the audience on the prevalence, rather than the undesirability, of that behavior."[2] How crazy does that sound? Preachers may be the instigators of the decline of the faith, by inadvertently giving attention to negative social proof week after week after week for generations.

Carl F. H. Henry stated, "The early Christians did not exclaim, 'What has the world come to?' Rather they proclaimed, "Look what has come to the world!'"[3] This is a fundamentally different way of reframing what God is doing in and around us. Instead of focusing so much on the negative, we focus on the glory of the gospel and how Christ is still moving in the world today, and doing this makes us influential in our culture.

Christians have become known more for what they are against than what they are for. And this is a problem, because we are not influential as Christians when we preach against the bad in culture. We are influential when we preach the good in Christ. Scripture calls us to focus on what is true, lovely, noble, and of good report (Phil. 4:8 NKJV). Psalm 33:5 tells us, "The LORD loves righteousness and justice; the earth is full of his unfailing love." It's important we realize that even though we encounter much pain and evil in our time on earth, it's just as important to recognize the earth is also full of the love, mercy, and goodness of God. Some people only see the bad, and that can be incredibly disheartening.

While the early Christians challenged problems in the church, their consistent message was, "The gospel is bearing fruit and growing throughout the whole world" (Col. 1:6). And this gospel is still growing and bearing fruit all over the world today. It's even growing and bearing fruit right in front of our noses.

Christians are losing influence in our culture because we've gotten sidetracked by secondary issues, such as theological differences and when and how to conduct a church service or ministry. When, and only when, we get back to the goodness, hope, joy, and love in the gospel and how God is using that gospel in the lives of people all around us will we have a powerful antidote for the deepest pains of our culture.

It is so important for church leaders and believers everywhere to change their own perspectives first. Begin by taking note of the great works God is doing around us and across the earth today: it will encourage us in our own faith in Christ, and it will direct our thoughts and our actions with a different, much needed set of "social proofs" that so many Christians are crying out for these days.

What If the Apostles Had Talked Like We Talk?

Remember that haunting question I asked myself recently: *What if the apostles had preached the way we preach these days?* By the way many talk in the pulpit about the church, our message may as well be something like "join our dying cause" or, as Carl F. H. Henry worded it, "What has the world come to?" If the apostles had preached this debilitating message, would any of us be saved? Would you or I be missing the glorious experience of knowing Christ many generations later?

When we look through the pages of Scripture, we see that the apostles clearly saw problems in church, but they still wrote of a glorious church. While they wrote to correct its problems, they also wrote of how Christianity was exploding everywhere. "The gospel is bearing fruit and growing throughout the whole world—just as it has been doing among you since the day you heard it and truly understood God's grace" (Col. 1:6).

When was the last time you heard a pastor preach about Christianity exploding around the world? When was the last time you thought about your own faith that way? People want to follow a glorious Savior and walk hand-in-hand with a glorious church, and we have more reason than any other institution or brand in the world today to speak of the glory of our cause.

People Are Starving for the Greatness of God

Dr. John Piper is the founder of Desiring God, a teaching ministry that has grown in less than two decades to become the most visited Christian blog in the world. He writes in his book *The Supremacy of God in Preaching*: "People are starving for the greatness of God. . . . Preaching that does not have the aroma of God's greatness may entertain for a season, but it will not touch the hidden cry of the soul: 'Show me thy glory!'"

Dr. Piper went on to share how, during the January prayer week at Bethlehem Baptist Church in Minneapolis, he made the decision to preach on the holiness of God from the passage found in Isaiah 6. Although he may normally follow messages with application, during that particular message he did not give one word of application. He "felt led that day to make a test: Would the passionate portrayal of the greatness of God in and of itself meet the needs of the people?"

Little did he realize that leading up to that service, a young family in the church discovered their child was being sexually abused by a relative. They were traumatized and heartbroken and didn't know how to cope. Weeks after the message of the holiness of God from Isaiah 6, with zero application, the husband of that family asked to speak with Dr. Piper and pulled him aside to share, "John, these have been the hardest months of our lives. Do you know what has gotten me through? The vision of the greatness of God's holiness that you gave me the first week of January. It has been the rock we could stand on." Dr. Piper concluded that "the greatness and the glory of God are relevant. It does not matter if surveys turn up a list of perceived needs that does not include the supreme greatness of the sovereign God of grace. That is the deepest need. Our people are starving for God."[4]

I agree with Dr. Piper: "People are starving for the greatness of God." And one of the primary ways we see the greatness of God is by recognizing his move on earth through his church and through his people. But it is so little recognized or discussed. If pastors don't know or care, how will people in our churches know or care? We will have a greater impact on the world around us when we notice how God is moving through the message of his Son, and we point to it and say: "Look what has come to the world!"

The Early Church Would Want What We Have

Some Christians talk about wanting to live in the time of the early church. They talk about its revivals, but they forget its riots.

The early church, with all its persecutions and challenges, could only dream of the opportunity we have in our time. They bore their sufferings in the hope and prayer of a better time; a time like ours in America today. They would be using this tremendous growth of the church through centuries and millennia to point to Christ and say, "Look what has come to the world!"

Many parts of the world today don't enjoy our religious freedoms, and yet even in those places, we see the gospel is bearing fruit and growing at a shocking rate. Let's be honest—the early church had way more reasons, statistically, to be depressed and discouraged than we do in America today. But somehow, they peered through a very different lens than ours. It is my great hope that we could also discover their lens and see the church and the world differently.

Divorce Rates among Christians

Maybe you are a well-meaning Christian and you cannot imagine trying to reframe the statistics. All you can see is the negative. You think you should just preach it as you see it and let the results rest in God. In some people's attempts to be honest and not lie about the state of the church, they actually end up not telling the truth.

One statistic I have heard more than a few times from church leaders in the pulpit and out of it is that divorce rates among Christians in America are the same as those of non-Christians. I heard this stated emphatically growing up. This statement is a great example of the lesson we learned from the Arizona Petrified National Park signage.

This statement, which has been made by multitudes of pastors and Christians, is in reality completely false. The Barna Group discovered that among those Americans claiming to practice the Christian faith, a smaller percentage actually practice and believe the basic, important tenants of the Christian faith.[5] *Of those who actually practice and believe the core tenants of the Christian faith, the divorce rate is significantly lower* than that of the nominal Christian and non-Christian populations. Why is this? Because they are too scared to divorce? No. Mostly because they are happier. Life works better when you work it God's way.

The Baptist Press confirms this reality:

> Professor Bradley Wright, a sociologist at the University of Connecticut, explains from his analysis of people who identify as Christians but rarely attend church, that 60 percent of these have been divorced. Of those who attend church regularly, 38 percent have been divorced. Other data from additional sociologists of family and religion suggest a significant marital stability divide between those who take their faith seriously and those who do not.[6]

Would you commit to the Christian faith if you thought it would cut your chances of divorce in half? Many might say yes, but no one is sharing these statistics. This is just one example of many that represents the widespread misuse and abuse of statistics by Christians and church leaders in our nation.

Does it really do us good to throw around negative statistics in the church? *As one of the few nations in human history in which the majority of the population claims faith in Christianity, are we really in a place to complain and look negatively on what is taking place around us?* And yet, somehow, people find a way to frame our circumstances so that it sounds like the world will end tomorrow. Will this kind of communicating really get us to a better place than where we are now? Especially when we haven't done our research and the statements we are making are wrong?

Maybe, by shedding light on young people leaving the church or speaking of divorce rates among Christians, preachers have inadvertently communicated a different message than they intended, and a young graduate or struggling couple receives the "proof" they needed from the pulpit to call it quits. We end up helping the very things we hate when we put the spotlight on our culture and its ills. We often actually end up promoting the wrong ideals as the norm. It's no wonder our youth are falling apart; they have heard about "the wrong things to do" all their lives.

The "All Wars Are Caused by Religion" Myth

Another example of statistical abuse is the commonly stated theory that many of the wars in history have resulted from religion and religious conflict. I haven't heard this statement stated by Christians, but I have heard it many times from atheists and nonbelievers, who supposedly all heard it from their college professors.

I never knew where this claim was coming from, and I didn't have any authoritative stance on it other than that I couldn't name more than one or two wars in particular that had anything to do with religion. Then I saw an online post from Lee Strobel.

Strobel, author of the bestselling *The Case for Faith* and other apologetics books, quotes the *Encyclopedia of Wars*, saying, "Of 1,763 major conflicts in recorded history, only 123 were fought over religious differences."[7] This is less than seven percent of major wars in history, accounting for just two percent of the casualties. Beyond this, we can safely assume that not all of those 123 wars had anything to do with Christians. And any Christians who did take innocent life in the name of faith are questionably Christian—by the majority of believing Christians around the world, anyway.

If only 123 wars in world history have originated in religion, compared to 1,640 caused for other reasons, maybe we all ought to give religion a try. Granted, while it is shocking to think faith in the loving Christian God would cause someone to fight another human, the reality is that even religiously moral people are not perfect—we all need more true religion based in God's love, not less.

True Christians, historically, have always been far more clearly seen to be the martyr rather than the oppressor. Indeed, Christians around the world on this very day are giving their lives rather than denying the gospel. The kind of statement that "all religion is good for is causing wars" is just one more example that has resulted in abuse after abuse and has turned well-meaning young believers from the faith, even though it is so seriously and fundamentally wrong.

News Often Results in More News

Malcom Gladwell shared recently in *RELEVANT* magazine that he rediscovered his Christian faith while writing his book *David and Goliath* after coming across a powerful example of forgiveness from a believer in Winnipeg, Canada. Gladwell's experience is a surprising and encouraging example of how God can use one believer's story to influence a hardened non-believer to God's story.

He writes in his book *The Tipping Point* about how what we share often creates ripple effects. In his research, he came across a study of shocking suicide rates on the islands of Micronesia in the early 1960s. It had been almost unheard of before that time, but for some reason, he shares, suicides on the islands of Micronesia "began to rise, steeply and dramatically, by leaps and bounds every year, until by the end of the 1980s there were more suicides per capita in Micronesia than anywhere else in the world." What was the cause? Anthropologist Donald Rubinstein relates that "as the number of suicides have grown, the idea has fed upon itself, infecting younger and younger boys, and transforming the act itself so that the unthinkable has somehow been rendered thinkable."[8]

The reality is that *what's on the news often makes more news*. News can stiffen the spines of others to follow suit, for good or peril. That's why what we magnify in our culture is important, and it's important what we magnify in the church.

Breaking the Four-Minute Mile Barrier

When something significant breaks loose, the knowledge of it can inspire even greater movements if the story gets out.

Take, for instance, the example of the 1954 World Olympics. On June 6, 1954, Roger Bannister broke a running record that many people of that day had presumed was impossible. He ran the mile in less than four minutes. "There were newspaper and television articles. Bannister's face was on magazine covers and cereal boxes. There were even rumors that he would be knighted by the queen." But his success was short lived. After all the centuries of people presuming the four-minute mile was impossible, only one month later another runner also broke the four-minute mile. "Soon a sub-four mile became less a miracle than an expectation of top runners. What had accelerated the pace? Recognition. Bannister's achievement had shown the rest of the pack what was possible."[9]

In both cases, for the good or for the bad, what we recognize and share with others can, and often does, cause a ripple effect. *"Bannister's achievement had shown the rest of the pack what was possible."*

A great many Christians have been impacted by reading the biographies or journals of men and women of faith through Christian history. Those testimonies show us what is possible—a level of faith that we can contend for.

How Nike Took Off Running

Speaking of running, my friend Harry Beckwith, author of one of the top ten bestselling business books of all time, *Selling the Invisible*, writes in another of his books, *What Clients Love*, about the story of Nike shoes. Nike began in Oregon track coach Bill Bowerman's kitchen. Together with Phil Knight, he worked to make a new and superior running shoe. During the 1972 Olympics in Germany, American marathon runner Frank Shorter claimed the victory. This "turned America, almost overnight, into a nation of runners . . . prompting Americans who had not run since PE class to jog a mile the next morning. Fortunately for Nike, these new converts needed shoes."[10]

People are social creatures who can be inspired, and when we foresee a "win" in a certain area of society, we tend to go with the flow and respond accordingly. We love to be inspired, and inspiration tends to move us along in the direction it dictates. In the same vein as Nike benefiting from Olympic records broken, the church benefits as the people of God see growth within the church and hear of the real-world impact of the church within the larger society.

What if there are spiritual records being broken today, and nobody knows about them? Will they have the impact God intended? Definitely not.

Paul the apostle most likely watched the ancient Roman games at some point, because he referred to our faith as a race: "I have fought the good fight, I have finished the race, I have kept the faith. Now there is in store for me the crown of righteousness, which the Lord, the righteous Judge, will award to me on that day—and not only to me, but also to all who have longed for his appearing" (2 Tim. 4:7–8). By running our own spiritual race well, we encourage others in their races. And by watching others race well for the Lord, we also get a second wind in our own races.

We need to stop pining and start proclaiming, "Look what has come to the world!"

Go to www.thinke.org for Challenge #8.

To Think About

1. What story speaks the most to you and why does it grip your heart?

2. In what ways have you been guilty of speaking negatively about the faith, and how can you correct this kind of thinking and speaking?

3. Do you believe we have opportunities and blessings that the first Christians would have dreamed of? How can we take advantage of these to further God's kingdom?

4. Like the Scripture says, how can you focus more on things that are lovely, pure, noble, and of good report?

Notes

[1] Robert Cialdini, *Yes!* (New York: Free Press, 2008), 21–23.

[2] Ibid, 21.

[3] Carl F. H. Henry, *The Christian Mindset In A Secular Society* (Portland: Multnomah Press, 1984), 34.

[4] John Piper, *The Supremacy of God in Preaching* (Grand Rapids: Baker Books, 2004), 13–14.

[5] Barna Group, Most American Christians Do Not Believe that Satan or the Holy Spirit Exist," *Barna Group,* April 10, 2009, https://www.barna.org/barna-update/faith-spirituality/260-most-american-christians-do-not-believe-that-satan-or-the-holy-spirit-exis#.VEh7nr5zGys.

[6] Glenn T. Stanton, "FIRST-PERSON: The Christian divorce rate myth (what you've heard is wrong)," *Baptist Press,* February 15, 2011, http://www.bpnews.net/34656.

[7] Lee Strobel, February 18, 2013, accessed October 28, 2014, https://twitter.com/LeeStrobel/status/303646526843023360.

[8] Malcolm Gladwell, *The Tipping Point* (New York: Little, Brown and Company, 2000), 216–218.

[9] Adrian Gostick and Chester Elton, *The Carrot Principle* (New York: Free Press, 2007), 20–21.

[10] Harry Beckwith, *What Clients Love* (New York: Business Plus, 2003), 6–7.

Chapter Nine

WHAT DOES GOD WANT FROM MY LIFE?

*God doesn't just want to save our souls;
he wants to move every area of our life on to
the path of godly wisdom and usefulness.*

—Matt Brown

My friend Zane speaks for Dare 2 Share youth conferences, which reach tens of thousands each year. He works with a guy named Greg, who founded these conferences. Greg reminds me of a modern-day Dwight L. Moody. Together, they are training the next generation to spread God's truth and love.

Zane came to Christ out of a life of drugs and ignorance to God. He writes in one of his books about his pre-Christ party days:

> Sin is fun. . . . People do it because at the time it
> seems fun, and it is. The Bible even recognizes that
> sin is fun. Hebrews 11:25 describes Moses as "choosing rather to be mistreated with the people of God
> than to enjoy the fleeting pleasures of sin." If you
> are honest, at some level, you too have enjoyed the

pleasures of sin . . . any sin. Because all sin entices us by claiming to bring fulfillment or joy, but always fails to deliver in the end. But like the Bible says, you have also probably found those pleasures to be fleeting.

It's like jumping off a building without a parachute. The first 100 feet is gonna be epic. But when the reality of the ground comes, you will find your epic free fall to have been short lived, with a terrible ending. . . .

All over the world, people chase after the pleasures of this world, seeking their own desires and end up unsatisfied. . . .

I was the same way, though. I could find nothing that fully satisfied.[1]

By God's grace, Zane discovered this satisfaction in Christ, which led him from Seattle, where he grew up, to studying at a small Bible school in Winter Park, Colorado, called Torchbearers. Torchbearers was started by a war veteran, Major Ian Thomas. Zane couldn't speak highly enough of his books, so I picked up a copy of the classic *Saving Life of Christ* and was deeply moved by the depth of discipleship within its pages.

Major Thomas shares, "All down the history of the church, every spiritual awakening and every mighty movement of God has been the consequence of a return to the basic teachings of the Bible, and inevitably, in reverse, such a genuine spiritual awakening has always produced Bible-believing Christians."[2] Awakening results from obedience to the Bible, and awakening produces obedience to the Bible. Our part is obedience, and God's part is to do what only he can do and awaken our eyes, ears, and hearts to his power and goodness.

Where Awakenings Are Rooted

When we see God move, it gives us faith in his Word. His Word, in turn, is the root of all the good things God wants to give us and show us. Like a good Father, God longs to usher us into what's best for us. His Word is our guide into his goodness and faithfulness.

Revival and awakening have historically been movements that only God can set into motion, but over and over again we see in God's Word and in history that God is extremely eager to move on our behalf. As we read and respond to his Word, he graciously pours out his Spirit and opens our eyes to his glory. Scripture reminds us, "If my people, who are called by my name, will humble themselves and pray and seek my face and turn from their wicked ways, then I will hear from heaven, and I will forgive their sin and will heal their land" (2 Chron. 7:14). This is not "those people out there," but "my people." That is you and me. God wants more from us, and when we give him more of us, he gladly gives us more of himself.

Often what we classify as real revival is only a small portion of the great revival and awakening that God is pouring out today in our culture, in churches globally, and in countless hearts and lives. Granted, some movements may seem more significant than others in our eyes, but the reality is that when the gospel goes forth and touches even one life and brings it from darkness to light—this is greater than any sign, wonder, revival, or awakening. The greatest miracle is always a soul finding Christ. There is nothing greater, nothing more important or urgent than this one task. My friend Brad Watson has said: "If you follow Jesus, you may never see revival, but you are guaranteed one thing: Jesus." And what a guarantee that is. In every sense, Jesus is revival: for every soul, for every heart. We may never see what some people classify as a "real revival" or a "great revival," but we have nothing to be sorrowful about if our souls are awakening to the Savior. We have something in the gospel that is greater than any of our wildest dreams—realized. We already have it in the gospel; it is already ours.

I want to wrap up with simple, important steps we can all take to live daily in the awakening of God's Spirit, to stay awake and inspired, and in turn to be influential for the sake of the gospel. These are takeaways from the stories we've studied together, and each one is vital as you seek God for your own community. My prayer is that these stories will live on in your story . . . that these stories will inspire and draw more to faith in the Savior.

Set Your Heart Apart for God for Life

We live in a day and age that has forgotten the "fear of the Lord." Scripture is crystal clear that the "fear of the Lord is the beginning of wisdom" (Prov. 9:10). Not the learning of human genius, but all true wisdom is rooted in the place of reverence and awe of God and his power. Think about it—who created the first university or the first doctorate program? People who didn't have a degree or a doctorate, but who decided in their human understanding that they had wisdom the rest of us needed. It is all man-made. We cannot honestly regard the wisdom of man that denies the fear of God as true wisdom.

But even while the carnal man denies God's truth, it remains as God's standard for those who would follow him.

> For the grace of God has appeared that offers salva-
> tion to all people. It teaches us to say "No" to ungod-
> liness and worldly passions, and to live self-controlled,

upright and godly lives in this present age, while we wait for the blessed hope—the appearing of the glory of our great God and Savior, Jesus Christ, who gave himself for us to redeem us from all wickedness and to purify for himself a people that are his very own, eager to do what is good. (Titus 2:11–14)

John, who walked closely with Jesus, teaches us to stay close to the Lord. "Dear children, keep away from anything that might take God's place in your hearts" (1 John 5:21 NLT).

Nothing can take the place of obedience to the Word of God. This is what sets us apart to be useful for God in the world. None of us is perfect, but that shouldn't stop us from trying to follow the Lord with all our hearts. There is a blessing from God for every commandment of God. The blessing of God follows adherence to the Word of God. R. A. Torrey said: "The power that belongs to God is stored up in the great reservoir of his own Word. Yet the Christians who pray for power, but neglect the Word abound in the church. If we are to obtain fullness of power in life and service, we must feed on the Word."[3]

Many Christians live passionate for God for a season; they obey God's Word for a season, but then they fizzle out. They need to make a decision, and that decision is to give their life to God. If we are going to give our lives to Christ, it will take a lifetime to fully do it, because we can only give our lives away over a lifetime.

Billy Graham gives us insight into the importance of obedience to God.

We in the church have failed to remind this generation that while God is love, He also has the capacity to hate. He hates sin, and He will judge it with the fierceness of His wrath. This generation is schooled in the teaching about an indulgent, softhearted God whose judgments are uncertain and who coddles those who break His commandments. This generation finds it difficult to believe that God hates sin.

I tell you that God hates sin just as a father hates a rattlesnake that threatens the safety and life of his child. God loathes evil and diabolic forces that would pull people down to a godless eternity just as a mother hates a venomous spider that is found playing on the soft, warm flesh of her little baby.

It is His love for man, His compassion for the human race, which prompts God to hate sin with such a vengeance. He gave Heaven's finest that we might have the best; and He loathes with a holy abhorrence anything that would hinder our being reconciled to Him.[4]

Let's trust that God calls us to obey for our good. When we obey, God blesses our obedience, and our spiritual vision is opened in greater ways. We see God is ultimately working for our good and his glory, and it gives us faith to trust and obey him even further. This cyclical effect builds into awakenings in hearts, families, cities, and even nations.

Let Your Graciousness Be Evident to All

Too often, we view righteousness and walking with Christ as a stringent, ascetic, angry path, when the truth is that kindness and humility are just as much a part of righteousness as setting apart our hearts to the Lord. Righteousness is not those things you don't do; righteousness is caring for others with the love God has shown you. The reality is that this is how you know if you're getting closer to God: more kindness, more gentleness, more joy, more peace, more patience. The fruit of the Holy Spirit is produced in our lives. We know we are growing closer to God if we are growing in grace and care for others, even those we do not want to care about naturally.

But too many Christians are too focused on being political activists and end-time dispensationalists than on loving others like Christ desires. Let me ask you: Are you more known for politicking or for reflecting Christ? We often get to make either a point or a difference, not both. It's really hard to be friends with people who always think they are right. Good friendships are built on give and take, so lay down any pride and simply care about people. Don't trumpet every problem you have with culture—instead trumpet the gospel, the great love of God in Christ for failing, struggling, desperate sinners. People won't find Christ because you expressed your frustration over politics. They will find Christ when you talk about the gospel.

Are you focused more on end-times prophecy than loving people and sharing the gospel of grace with graciousness? While every Christian has different areas God burdens their heart for, the primary calling of every believer is to look like Jesus, not an angry prophet from the Old Testament. And what did Jesus do? He loved the sinner so visibly that people called him a friend of sinners. *Could anyone accuse you of that?* Hopefully, we grow in prioritizing caring for people over making a point, like Jesus did. His ways are so counterintuitive to our human nature. He calls us to different things than our hearts naturally bend toward.

Christians who choose intensity over nonessentials, rather than unity with, and honoring of, other believers, don't understand the heart of God. I heard about a Christian in the Twin Cities who was so upset that General Mills supported gay marriage that he protested by burning boxes of Cheerios on the corporation's front lawn. Within a week, he passed away from a heart attack. James tell us, "For a man's anger does not lead to action which God regards as righteous" (James 1:20 WNT). And Paul tells us, "Do everything without grumbling or arguing, so that you may become blameless and pure, 'children of God without fault in a warped and crooked generation.' Then you will shine among them like stars in the sky as you hold firmly to the word of life" (Phil. 2:14–16). If we are going to shine for Christ, we have to be filled with the kindness of Christ.

Does the following list sound like you? This is what the Bible calls us to.

- "Let your speech always be gracious" (Col. 4:6 NRSV).
- "If it is possible, so far as it depends on you, live peaceably with all" (Rom. 12:18 NRSV).
- "[Share the gospel] with gentleness and respect" (1 Pet. 3:15b).

Honor What God Is Doing through Others

Our first time at Catalyst Conference in Atlanta was mind-blowing—thirteen thousand people, mostly young pastors and leaders, converging to grow in God and become more effective in ministry. Michelle and I, in the midst of being in awe over what God was doing at the conference, sat out on the lawn for lunch on the second day, along with a few friends. One friend brought another friend to meet us who hadn't been at the conference that year (but had attended in past years). He spent the entire hour of our lunch meeting declaring how God was done moving in big ways in big crowds and big churches, how the effectiveness of megachurches was waning, and on and on and on. All this on the front lawn of Catalyst Conference in Atlanta, where thousands of pastors of thousands of growing, thriving mega-churches were convened and praying together that God would increase their efforts. I'm not kidding; you can't make this stuff up. After about forty-five minutes, I couldn't handle it anymore, and I openly told him we rejected his statements. Don't get me wrong, he was a wonderful believer, doing wonderful things for God in his city; it's just that he didn't want to believe there was anything wonderful happening outside himself.

This is not the way God wants us to be. Please, please, please get excited about what God is doing outside of your own church and ministry. Please show honor to what God is doing in other places. We need to stop saying things like, "God can't use out-reaches anymore. No one actually gets saved, they just pray a prayer," and "Megachurches are ineffective and lack community and accountability," or "These are the ways this leader or minis-try gets it wrong." The reality is that these statements are often just plain false. We need to stop letting underlying jealousy and negativity in our spirit come out in a way that tears down what God is doing with others. Instead, train yourself to rejoice at any little thing God is doing in any little place, and any big thing God is doing in any big place. Honor it. Thank God for it. Ask God to do it again in your own community. "Won't you revive us again, so your people can rejoice in you?" (Ps. 85:6 NLT).

I love the story of Elijah in the Old Testament. In 1 Kings 18, Elijah complains to a crowd that he is the only prophet of God left. Shortly afterward, he complains multiple times to God in prayer this same sentiment: "I have been very zealous for the LORD God Almighty. The Israelites have rejected your covenant, torn down your altars, and put your prophets to death with the sword. *I am the only one left*, and now they are trying to kill me too" (19:10; italics mine). God proceeds to call Elijah to the face of the mountain and appears to him in mighty wind, earthquake, and fire and eventually in the form of a whisper.

Many Christians have repeated this story, and they love this idea that God speaks to us today in the form of a whisper, but we forget what was whispered. Here it is: "Yet I reserve seven thousand in Israel—all whose knees have not bowed down to Baal and whose mouths have not kissed him" (1 Kings 19:18). God's whisper to Elijah was that there was far more happening beyond what he had been saying or seeing. Thousands had been set apart for the Lord and his purposes and were activated in their own communities. For all Elijah's seven thousand, there are millions upon millions set apart all over the world today. And God wants to whisper this into our spirits, so we never forget. *God is writing a bigger story, but so many of us are focusing on one letter of one word of one line of one chapter.* Let's honor the rest of God's story, the story he is working outside of our smaller stories, the story he is working out in others.

Build Your Life around the Gospel

Therefore, since we are surrounded by such a great cloud of witnesses, let us throw off everything that hinders and the sin that so easily entangles. And let us run with perseverance the race marked out for us, fixing our eyes on Jesus, the pioneer and perfecter of faith. For the joy set before him he endured the cross, scorning its shame, and sat down at the right hand of the throne of God. Consider him who endured such opposition from sinners, so that you will not grow weary and lose heart. (Heb. 12:1–3)

Let's fix our eyes on Jesus. Matt Chandler has said, "The gospel not only saves us, the gospel also sustains us."[5] We all need to preach the gospel to our own hearts every single day. It's important to often remind our own hearts and minds of the gospel. The gospel is not something that saves us and then we move on. Every day we are in need of the grace of Jesus Christ and the work he finished on the cross.

The gospel also reminds us that we are alive and loved because of God's finished work on the cross, once for all, not by our constant work for God. We work from a place of rest and completion. The gospel shows us that God cares more than we do, and everything he asks us to do he has already done more for us first. *To the extent we enjoy a rich, satisfying relationship with Jesus and treasure his gospel—that is the extent to which we will draw others to the gospel.* This should be our first priority—contemplating and enjoying and building our lives around the gospel.

But sometimes we build our lives around a religion of morality—around the work we do for Jesus, instead of the work he has already done for us. My great-grandfather was guilty of this. For years he traveled and pastored Methodist churches around Canada. After many years, toward the end of his ministry, he wrote in his journal his deep regret that for years he had preached morality—for people to do better and try harder, rather than the gospel of Jesus's finished work on the cross for our sins—and trusting Christ alone for salvation. We negate the power of the cross, and we exhaust ourselves when we try to live up to a standard that Christ already fulfilled for us on the cross. *Good works do not set us apart from any other religion in the world. Christ alone is the difference.* Let's build our lives on Christ alone. "For it is by grace you have been saved, through faith; and this is not from yourselves, it is the gift of God" (Eph. 2:8).

Building our lives around the gospel also means we work to make much of the gospel over all other theology. I grew up in charismatic circles within the church, and while it is wonderful to talk about God's power, are we known most for miracles (or some other distinctive theology) or for the gospel? Too often we highlight what makes us different from other Christians, when we should be making much of Jesus.

Jesus says in Mark 16:17 (NKJV) that "these signs will follow those who believe," but some Christians read it in reverse, that "those who believe will follow these signs." *Are you following signs, or are signs following you?* In my personal study of George Whitfield, John Wesley, Dwight L. Moody, and other leaders' journals and biographies, I discovered that many of them saw interesting miracles happen at some point in their ministries, but they didn't overemphasize this—they emphasized Christ. They kept their focus on Christ. Jesus himself didn't proclaim miracles; he did miracles, and he proclaimed the kingdom. We all have to be mindful and careful what we emphasize the most when we represent our faith.

Endure Hardships for Christ

Just because God is moving does not mean we won't encounter hardships. In the book of Acts, God moved a lot, but there were also an incredible number of obstacles, hardships, persecutions, and pains. Paul taught the early church: "We must go through many hardships to enter the kingdom of God" (Acts 14:22).

Even though our hearts are awakened to see God's activity and inspired by all that he is doing, there will always be a sense within our hearts that all is not right with the world. This world is not our home, and for followers of Christ, it will never feel like it is our home. Author Dave Arnold works with refugees and displaced peoples when they arrive in America, and he explains from the refugee perspective this sense of longing in the Christian for our true home in heaven:

For years I too attempted to push away my ache through working, attempting to find my identity and significance through what I did, or what people expected of me, or what I thought God expected of me. But no matter how much we do for God, how many people we seek to please, or how busy we are, the ache remains—a feeling that something is not right in our world, or more substantially, something's not right in us. It's the story we find ourselves in. The ache remains. Indeed it must remain. . . . What we long for, what we are made for, lies in the future.[6]

Paul writes in his final letter in Scripture, "Now there is in store for me the crown of righteousness, which the Lord, the righteous Judge, will award to me on that day—and not only to me, but also to all who have longed for his appearing" (2 Tim. 4:8). We are people who long for Christ's appearing—we long for heaven. We long to be in the place of perfection, because this earth does not satisfy. We have tasted of God's goodness and Holy Spirit, and we long to be made complete and whole in his presence. We long for heaven. Do you long for heaven? Do you long for Christ? Do you long to be done with sickness, pain, tragedy, and death? God has put eternity in our hearts, and this world will never satisfy, so we cry out with the psalmist, "As the deer longs for streams of water, so I long for you, O God" (Ps. 42:1 NLT).

Share What God Is Showing You

John 7:38 says, "Whoever believes in me, as Scripture has said, rivers of living water will flow from within them." Living water is a reference to those times, as a flowing water source that is continually moving. Still water (think of a bird bath) would eventually grow stagnant and smelly and need to be replaced. Living water refers to a river that keeps moving and thus stays fresh and clean. What this means to the believer is that when God does something in your life, keep it moving by allowing it to touch and bless others around you—share what God is doing in your heart.

If this book has encouraged your faith, I want to encourage you to pass the book on to others. Pass on any excitement that you have about the things of God. Bring others into the experience. Allow the refreshment God has poured into your soul to flow through you into many other lives. Allow it to be Living Water within and flowing through you. As you pour it out to others, God will always pour more into you.

Find a Need and Fill It

Finally, it is my great hope that each one of the stories in this book would serve to inspire you for what God might be speaking to you individually today. My dream is that these stories would awaken and inspire action in you to be influential for the kingdom of God. God has a good plan for each one of us. This plan begins with making much of his Son, and moves on to you helping others see the goodness and reality of God in this generation.

The Bible tells us, "He who did not spare his own Son, but gave him up for us all—how will he not also, along with him, graciously give us all things?" (Rom. 8:32). God will take care of you, and I believe he will also give you opportunities to serve and be influential for him.

I pray this is not a vision of how you can be great, but a vision of how you can serve others; a vision of how you can bless others with the same love that God has so graciously blessed you with in sending his Son as a sacrifice for your sins. Maybe

God is speaking to you as you read this book that you are on the right track. Maybe he is saying to keep on the same path, and you are feeling greater joy and purpose in what you already know you are called to do. That is wonderful. Often it is not your trajectory that needs to change but your perspective—this can make all the difference.

However, maybe God is telling you to change some things, or he is giving you a heart or a plan to step out into greater things he has for you to do. It is so important to keep an open and willing heart to whatever God wants you to do. God will make his will known in your life. You don't have to worry that a random passing thought to sell everything and move to Africa will ruin your life. God often speaks in an echo—the same thought, impression, Scripture, or direction is given over and over again and grows in your spirit until you know it is clearly from him. He will guide you. Trust him.

So here's to you. May you live fully awakened and inspired by God's work all around you, and be influential for the sake of the gospel. This is my prayer for you and for all whom you will influence.

Go to www.thinke.org for the final exercise, Challenge #9.

To Think About

1. What has God shown you through the course of reading this book?

2. What are one or two specific actions you know you need to put into practice to live influentially for God?

3. How can you keep your heart awakened to God's activity around the world?

4. Who else do you know who needs to read this book and hear these encouraging stories? (Consider doing a book study with a group of friends who would be encouraged by the book.)

Notes

[1] Zane Black, *InZane* (Arvada, CO: D2S Publishing, 2012), 30–32. Used with permission of author.

[2] Ian Thomas, *Saving Life of Christ* (Grand Rapids: Zondervan, 1961), 128.

[3] R. A. Torrey, *God's Power in Your Life* (New Kensington, PA: Whitaker House, 1982), 13.

[4] Billy Graham, "Things God Hates," *Decision*, August 25, 2011, http://billygraham.org/decision-magazine/september-2011/things-god-hates.

[5] Matt Chandler in the foreword of *Gospel Centered Discipleship* by Jonathan K. Dodson. (Wheaton, Illinois: Crossway Publishers, 2012.), 11.

[6] Dave Arnold, *Pilgrims in the Alley* (Portland: Urban Loft Publishers, 2013), 19.